CONQUERING CASINO CRAPS

CONQUERING CASINO CRAPS

JOHN GOLLEHON

CARDOZA PUBLISHING
Las Vegas, Nevada

Cardoza Publishing is the foremost gaming and gambling publisher in the world with a library of more than 200 up-to-date and easy-to-read books and strategies. These authoritative works are written by the top experts in their fields and with more than 10,000,000 books in print, represent the best-selling and most popular gaming books anywhere.

NEW EDITION!

New Edition Copyright© 1994, 1997, 2005, 2012 by John Gollehon
-All Rights Reserved-

Library of Congress Catalog Card No: 2011933350
ISBN 13: 978-1-5804-2297-0
ISBN 10:   1-5804-2297-7

Hurry up and visit our website or write for a full list of Cardoza Publishing books and advanced strategies.

CARDOZA PUBLISHING

P.O. Box 98115, Las Vegas, NV 89193
Phone (800)577-WINS
email: cardozabooks@aol.com
www.cardozabooks.com

About The Author

John Gollehon is considered more than just an expert player; he is a trusted authority, having written extensively on all the games included in this book. Gollehon is recognized by the national media as an expert on casino gambling and is frequently cited in newspaper stories on gaming. He has also appeared on numerous television documentaries. Gollehon's writings span five decades, having first published a gaming newsletter in 1979. He is the author of 28 titles on beating the casino, many of them best-sellers.

In his books, Gollehon shows players the skills they need to build confidence and become a top player, teaching them the secrets of developing timing—when to lay back, and when to deliver that knock-out punch.

Cardoza Books by John Gollehon
Conquering Casino Craps
Commando Craps & Blackjack!
Casino Games
What Casinos Don't Want You to Know
Attack the Casino's Vulnerable Games

To all craps shooters…
my friends on the battlefield

When you play,
play with caution,
play with patience.
You can't win
without them.
—John Gollehon

From The Author...

The decision to gamble is a personal one. It should take into account many things, not the least of which is your ability to wisely manage money. If you frequently overdraw your checking account, exceed your credit-card limits, or otherwise spend your money recklessly—buying on impulse, for example—suffice to say gambling is a bad idea.

If you do decide to try your luck, promise yourself that you will stay within your means. Playing craps can be fun. Don't let serious losses take your fun away.

Acknowledgments

Grateful appreciation is expressed to the following for their valued assistance in preparing the chapters on Power Shooters and Casino Countermeasures: Ron Asher, Chief of Enforcement, Nevada Gaming Control Board, Richard (Jerry) Clark, Surveillance Director, Caesars Palace, Las Vegas, George Joseph, Surveillance Director, Bally's, Las Vegas, Larry Dennison, Surveillance Director, Fitzgerald's, Reno, Dick Favero, Casino Manager, Palace Station, Las Vegas. A special "thank you" to Jerry Clark for taking the time to review first drafts of the chapters.

T TABLE OF CONTENTS

TABLE OF CONTENTS

1 INTRODUCTION

People often ask me why I play craps—almost exclusively now among the table games—when they know I played blackjack successfully for years.

The truth is, I haven't given blackjack the time I used to because I no longer have the positive anticipation that kept me playing. In prior years, I felt confident I could beat the game with at least a modicum of consistency. Today, I have reservations. The casino's widely publicized countermeasures against skilled players have really dampened my interest. It's hard to maintain a level of confidence in blackjack, let alone any endeavor, when you know your opponent can disarm you on a whim!

Another reason I've moved to the dice tables is perhaps only a psychological one, but an important one: If I'm going to satisfy my anticipation of a large win, I know it's going to happen at a dice table. Not blackjack, not roulette, not slots, not keno, not poker, not baccarat. I am, however, comfortable with my anticipations in the casino's race and sports books— very comfortable—but my guts tell me that if I'm ever to walk away with chips falling out of my pockets, I'll be walking away from a 30-minute shoot at a bloodied dice table. And I've experienced many.

What I like most about this game is its uncanny nature of producing streaks. And for me, at least, there's a certain mystical quality that begs to be listened to. Part of the lure is actually built into the game itself: a natural streak-producing design based on the odds of a 7. Although a 7 is a winner at the start of a new hand, most of the time the 7 is a loser, as you'll soon learn.

The pure essence of the game is to roll either a 7 or 11 to win; a 2, 3, or 12 loses. Any other number becomes the shooter's point number, and it must be rolled again before a 7 is rolled in order to win. But the real calling of craps is how many numbers can be rolled while the shooter is trying for the point number. And, depending on how one goes about betting the game, those numbers that roll produce profits. The more numbers, the more profits.

Players are hunting for a hot shooter who can string together number after number. Craps is the hunt for the hot hand.

For those who have the discipline for this risky game, the reward is an incredible short-term potential.

2 THE BASICS

THE COME-OUT ROLL, PASS & DON'T PASS BETS

Craps is a simple game to play, but that doesn't mean it's easy to explain. Almost any explanation seems to overly complicate it.

To best understand the game, let's start with the **come-out roll**, the roll made before any point is established. All bets for the come-out roll are made on either the "pass line" or "don't pass line." The lines run along the entire table and it is here, on the lines directly in front of you, where you and other players at the table place your bet. We'll stick with just the pass line for now, since that's far and away the most popular bet.

A bet on the **pass line** means you are betting that the shooter does indeed win, which is called making a **pass**, by rolling either a 7 or 11 (a **natural**) for an immediate win, or by rolling a 4, 5, 6, 8, 9, or 10 (a **point number**) and then repeating that number before a 7 is rolled. If a 2, 3, or 12 (a **craps**) is rolled on the come out, the pass line loses.

2-3-12	7-11	4-10	5-9	6-8
Craps	Natural	Point numbers		
(Loser)	(Winner)	(Must be repeated to win)		

It's important to remember the point numbers in the pairs as I've listed them. You'll find out why later in this chapter.

If the shooter rolls a point number on the come out—let's say it's a 6—only the numbers 6 and 7 become relevant numbers to the pass line. All other numbers have no bearing. The shooter tosses the dice as many times as necessary until either one of those two numbers is made. Should the shooter roll a 7 and lose, it's called a **seven-out**. Not only does the pass line lose, the shooter also loses the dice and they are passed on to the next player, who becomes the shooter.

As you can see, it's a game where all the players on the pass line are teamed up and cheering for the win. When the pass line wins, everyone on the line wins! Unlike blackjack, the pass line presents a united effort to beat the house. Blackjack's only similarity is when everyone is rooting for the dealer to bust. A bust is a win for all the players, at least for those who didn't bust beforehand. But one thing you'll find at the dice tables that you rarely see (or should I say, "hear") at blackjack tables is a let-yourself-go, yell-and-scream excitement as you root for the shooter to win. A win, not surprisingly, is more exciting when everyone wins.

There is always a come-out roll right after a decision on the pass line. The dealers generally announce the come out by saying, "The dice are coming out," or, simply, "Coming out." There is always a come-out roll right after a shooter:

1. Makes the point number
2. Fails to make the point number (by rolling a seven-out)
3. Rolls a natural, or
4. Rolls a craps

If the shooter establishes a point number on the come out—the most likely scenario since it happens 66 percent of the time—players do not have to just stand around twiddling their fingers as they wait for a decision. Indeed not. As I alluded to earlier, the action on the table while a shooter is going for a point number is the real heat of the game. Some players elect to bet the remaining five point numbers with place bets, while others decide to make come bets. We'll talk about place bets later because they are not the recommended action to take. Come bets, however, represent the front line of huge battles won at the dice tables, so that's what we want to learn how to do.

THE COME BET

There's a big section at each end of the dice table labeled COME, and that's where come bets are made. Both ends of the table have identical layouts, so it makes no difference where you position yourself.

If you think of a **come bet** as a delayed pass line bet, it will be easier to understand. Let's say you have a $5 chip on the pass line and the shooter rolls the point of 5. If that's all you want to bet, that's fine, but if not, plunk down another nickel in the come and you've got another bet going. On the next roll, a 7 or 11 wins the come bet, a 2, 3, or 12 loses it, and you know the routine—any other number becomes the point number and it must be repeated before a 7 is rolled in order to win.

Let's say the next roll is a 9. Now you've got two numbers working for you. To make it easy for you to keep track of your come bet, the dealer will pick up your chip and place it in the corresponding **point box**. In this case, the point box 9. Since other players might be making come bets at the same time as you do, your chip will be positioned in the box relative to your position at the table. An easy way to tell your chip from the others in the box is to reference where you are standing in relation to the corner of the table.

Think of the corner of the box as representing the corner of the table. If you are standing at the front of the table, your bet will be along the front of the box. If you are standing at the end of the table, your bet will be along the back of the box. Most dice tables allow room for eight players at each end of the table—four along the front and four around the side. The point boxes are sized so that the dealer can place four bets across the front of the box and four bets across the back to account for all eight positions at that end of the table.

If the shooter makes your come bet number, the dealer will pick up the come bet and replace it in the come along with your even-money winnings on the bet. You must pick up the chips immediately, otherwise they are all in action as another come bet on the next toss. If you want to have a come bet for that next roll, you can simply pick up a portion of your payoff, leaving the remaining chips in the come for your next come bet.

OFF & ON

You can make as many come bets as you want. It's likely, if you are making a lot of them, that you will have a bet sitting in the come at the same time you have a come bet in one of the five remaining point boxes for which a point number has just rolled. Although there are six point boxes—one for each point number—only five remain since one of the numbers is the pass line point number. If both bets are the same amount, the dealer will simply pay you the winnings on the come bet by placing these winning chips in the come directly beside your bet in the come. This action is called **off and on** and is simply to make the game proceed more efficiently.

If your bet in the come is not at the same amount as your come bet in a winning point box, then the action is a bit more detailed: The dealer will first return your come bet to the come along with the winnings. The dealer will then pick up your bet in the come and place it in that same point box. The end effect is that you have increased the amount of the bet in that particular point box.

PLAYING THE GAME

Let's say the shooter is going after a point number. You have a pass line bet, two come bets in the point boxes, and another come bet sitting in the come. For the sake of discussion, let's say all of your bets are $5 (a **nickel**). Now, let's play the game:

The next roll of the dice is an 11. The dealer will pay you $5 in winnings for the come bet sitting in the come because it's a come-out roll for that particular bet. You pick up your nickel in winnings and leave a nickel in the come. The next roll of the dice is a 7. Your pass line bet loses, your two come bets in the point boxes lose, but your come bet sitting in the come wins again because it's still coming out.

Had the shooter rolled the pass line point number instead, you would have gotten paid $5 on the pass line, and your bet sitting in the come would have moved to that particular point box. At that point, you would have had three come bets in action for the next roll, which would be the come-out roll for the pass line.

If the shooter would then roll a 7, your pass line bet would win, but what would happen to your three come bets? For those bets, the 7 would be a seven-out and they would all lose. You can quickly see why 7s are particularly bad for multiple bet players. Sevens wipe out all the come bets sitting in the point boxes. Sevens only win on come out bets on the pass line and in the come.

Incidentally, when you walk up to a dice table, how do you know whether or not the shooter is about to make a come-out roll or is busy going after a point number?

Easy question. Easy answer.

Part of the equipment used on a dice table is a round puck, white on one side with the word ON in the center, and black on the other side with the word OFF in the center. When the shooter is going after a point number, the dealers will position this puck (actually two pucks, one for each end of the table) in the appropriate point box with the white side up. If the shooter is coming out, the puck will be positioned away from the point boxes (in an area reserved for don't come bets—don't ask about them now—with the black "OFF" side up. Now, if only the rest of the game were that easy to explain.

PROBABILITIES

Based on what we've just covered, it would seem as if this game is a cinch. There are only three ways to lose outright, with a 2, 3, or 12 craps. There are two ways to win outright with a 7 or 11, and even if you roll a point number all you have to do is roll it again to win, barring a 7, of course. Doesn't seem like a big deal, does it?

Well, it is a big deal because all the numbers that can come up from 2 to 12 have varying probabilities. And which number, do you suppose, is the most likely to come up?

Duh... 7?

Good guess.

Probability Chart

NUMBER	WAYS	PROBABILITY	HOW
2	1	35 to 1	1-1
3	2	17 to 1	1-2, 2-1
4	3	11 to 1	2-2, 1-3, 3-1
5	4	8 to 1	1-4, 4-1, 2-3, 3-2
6	5	6.2 to 1	3-3, 2-4, 4-2, 1-5, 5-1
7	6	5 to 1	1-6, 6-1, 2-5, 5-2, 3-4, 4-3
8	5	6.2 to 1	4-4, 2-6, 6-2, 3-5, 5-3
9	4	8 to 1	3-6, 6-3, 4-5, 5-4
10	3	11 to 1	5-5, 4-6, 6-4
11	2	17 to 1	5-6, 6-5
12	1	35 to 1	6-6
	36		

If you study the chart, you'll quickly see that it's easy to remember the spread of probabilities over the 36 different combinations by simply grouping the numbers. For example, both the 2 and 12 are the toughest to make because there is only one way in 36 to roll either number. One in 36 means the odds are 35 to 1. The numbers 3 and 11 come next, and so on, in groups of two.

You can memorize the odds for all the groups of numbers if you like, but it really isn't important for the particular bets we will be making. We are only interested in the lowest percentage bets available. And that, my friend, conveniently eliminates most of the bets and a lot of remembering.

See, I told you this wouldn't be too tough. Only three groups of numbers, the point numbers, are worth remembering, and they should always be remembered in the pairs as I've listed them.

As you can see, the odds of making the 4 or 10 are 11 to 1; the odds of making the 5 or 9 are 8 to 1; and the odds of making the 6 or 8 are a little more than 6 to 1. Clearly, the 5 to 1 odds of rolling a 7 are far and away the best odds of any number.

But the odds of rolling these numbers are not that important either, at least not to the particular bets we will want to make. What are important, however, are the odds of rolling these point numbers before rolling a 7.

POINT NUMBER	CORRECT ODDS OF REPEATING BEFORE A 7
6 & 8	6 to 5
5 & 9	3 to 2
4 & 10	2 to 1

Now we're getting somewhere.

If your point number is 4 (or 10), the odds that you will repeat the 4 before you roll a 7 are 2 to 1. If your point number is 5 (or 9), the odds that you will repeat the 5 before you roll a 7 are 3 to 2. And, if your point number is 6 (or 8), the odds that you will repeat the 6 before you roll a 7 are 6 to 5.

THE ODDS BET

Now that you understand the odds of rolling these point numbers before rolling a 7, we can talk about the third and last bet we will want to make. It's called an "odds bet," and it can be made along with both the pass line bet and come bet that we've already learned.

The pass line bet and come bet sport a modest percentage against you of just 1.41 percent. That's one of the lowest percentage bets you can make in the casino. But listen to this: The odds bet is paid off at *true odds*, not at even money! If you make the 4, for example, the odds bet will be paid off at 2 to 1 odds. That's 2 to 1 for your money! Bet $10 in odds and if the 4 hits you'll get a tidy payoff of $20!

Because the odds bet is paid off at true odds, there is no percentage advantage to the house! The odds bet at the dice tables is the only "fair" bet in the casino! It's obviously a bet that you must make.

To make this bet on the pass line, simply place the odds bet directly behind the pass line bet when a point number has been established. To make this bet on the come, simply place your odds bet in the come beside your come bet and announce to the dealer "Odds on my come bet." If the dealer is faster than you are and has already moved your come bet to the point box—let's say it went to the 9—simply place your odds bet in that same area of the come where your come bet was made and announce, "Odds on my 9." It's important that the dealer hears your instruction. Watch to make sure the dealer does, in fact, move your odds bet out of the come, otherwise he may mistake it for another come bet.

The dealer, incidentally, will position your odds bet on top of your come bet, but slightly offset to distinguish the two bets.

That's all there is to it! It's called **taking odds** and, as I said, any astute crapshooter knows that it's a bet you can't afford not to make.

ODDS BET PAYOFFS

The pass line bets and come bets are called **flat wagers**. The odds bet is simply called **odds**. If you recall, you are paid even money on all of your flat wagers, and now you've just learned that your odds is paid at the true probability of rolling a point number before rolling a 7.

What a deal!

To make it easy for the dealers to pay you on your odds bets (and we do want to make it easy for them), you must be sure that the odds bets can be paid off in even multiples of the odds. For example: Since the odds payoff on the 5 or 9 is 3 to 2, your odds bet must be divisible by 2. Since the odds payoff on the 6 or 8 is 6 to 5, it must be divisible by 5. The point numbers 4 and 10 with payoffs of 2 to 1 are no problem since everything is divisible by 1.

Let's say your odds bet is $10. If the point number that wins is 4, the payoff at 2 to 1 is $20. If the point number that wins is 5, the payoff at 3 to 2 is $15. If the point number that wins is 6, the payoff at 6 to 5 is $12.

It's easy to figure it out. On the payoff for the point numbers of 5 or 9, simply think how many times 2 goes into $10 and then multiple by 3. Dealers are taught to make the calculation on the 5 and 9 by expressing the odds as "odds to 1." So, 3 to 2 odds expressed as "odds to 1" are 1-1/2 to 1. If you bet $10, simply multiply the bet by 1-1/2.

For the 6 and 8, dealers are taught to express the odds as "odds to 10." So, 6 to 5 odds expressed as "odds to 10" are 12 to 10. For every $10, you get $12. But sometimes players make odds bets in odd numbers, such as $35. If the point is 6 or 8, most dealers will just think of the bet as earning an additional $7 for a $42 payoff. Their quick thinking is, "For every $5 bet, the player wins an extra dollar."

Regardless of how you decide to figure it, practice it every so often, especially before a gambling trip. You'll feel more confident in your betting if you know the payoffs for the different point numbers and know how to compute them.

And you should do it routinely at the table. Don't rely on the dealers to pay you correctly. They do make mistakes. A good player should be able to confirm that the payoff is accurate, and should get into the habit of doing this basic chore every time.

Incidentally, if you ever think your payoff is not correct, do not pick up your chips. Leave them on the table and tell the dealer you would like the payoff checked. Once you pick up your chips, the payoff stands.

Multiple Odds

Since the odds bet is such a favorable bet, the logical question has to be: How much odds can I take? And the answer depends on where you play. Years ago, most all casinos would only allow a player to take odds up to the amount of the flat wager. If you bet $5 on the pass line, your odds bet could be no more than $5. And it became a dice-table standard for many years—a $5 pass line bet or come bet with $5 odds, or $10 with $10, or $20 and $20 behind it. It was called **single odds.**

Then, in the early '80s, casinos began experimenting with **double odds.** A $5 bet on the pass line would allow you to wager $10 in odds behind it. It became an instant hit with dice players, as you might imagine. Soon, all casinos were offering double odds in order to stay competitive with the casino across the street.

The end effect of making the odds bet is that it lowers the overall percentage against you when both the flat wager and odds bet are taken into account. The 1.41 percent house advantage on just the flat wager is reduced to .83 percent with single odds, and reduced even further to .61 percent with double odds.

Today, you'll find casinos that offer three-times odds, some offer ten-times odds, and still other casinos are hawking 100-times odds. But, unlike that period in the '80s when all casinos had to match the competition, you'll find that most casinos stick with either double or triple odds. That seems to be good enough for most players.

Not surprisingly, when you play at better than double odds—five-times or ten-times, for example—the effect on the overall percentages becomes less remarkable. My recommendation has always been to use multiple odds as a progressive increase as you continue winning.

Clearly, if you choose to play at a time when the dice are not passing, high multiple odds will only result in a quicker exit.

Always begin with double odds and, if offered, go to three-times, then four-times, and so on, as you continue to win.

What you've just learned are the three best bets at the dice table. Of course, this doesn't mean that you'll win more times than not by making only these bets. It does mean that over the long term you will show better results than players who make the higher percentage bets.

We'll talk about them briefly in the following section, but I do not recommend that you even consider such bets.

OTHER BETS

Place bets are the next most common bet at the dice tables. Place bets allow you to bet any point number of your choosing without having to wait for it to hit on the come. The bets vary in percentages from 1.52 percent for placing the 6 or 8 (not a bad percentage, and sometimes good players make this bet) to over 6 percent for placing the 4 and 10. The chart that follows shows most of the other bets you can make at a dice table. I've included it here strictly for information purposes.

BET	PAYS	SHOULD PAY	CASINO ADVANTAGE
Any 7	4 to 1	5 to 1	16.67%
Any Craps	7 to 1	8 to 1	11.1%
11 (or 3)	15 to 1	17 to 1	11.1%
2 (or 12)	30 to 1	35 to 1	13.89%
Hard 6 (or 8)	9 to 1	10 to 1	9.1%
Hard 4 (or 10)	7 to 1	8 to 1	11.1%
Place 6 (or 8)	7 to 6	6 to 5	1.52%
Place 5 (or 9)	7 to 5	3 to 2	4.0%
Place 4 (or 10)	9 to 5	2 to 1	6.67%

Among all the other bets you can make, I want you to know here and now that the most tempting bets at the dice tables are called "hardways" and "elevens." "Any craps" bets on the come out are nearly as contagious. I'm sure it comes as no surprise to you that these bets are also among the highest percentage bets against you. Indeed, these forbidden fruits of the dice table are gobbled down in sheer gluttony by players who either don't know better, or don't care.

Hardways represent the point numbers that can be made "hard": 4, 6, 8, and 10. Making these numbers **hard** means making them in pairs, such as 2-2 for the 4, and 3-3 for the 6. Your bet wins if the number is made hard, and loses if the number is made **easy** (any other way, such as 3-1 for the 4) or if a 7 is rolled.

The **eleven** bet, like the any craps bet, is a one-roll bet usually made on the come out. You win if an 11 is thrown; you lose on any other number. Same goes for the **any craps** bets. If any craps number, 2, 3, or 12, is rolled on the come out, you win. You lose on any other number. Of course, these bets can be made anytime but are most commonly seen during the come out.

BEING A TOUGH PLAYER

I assume that since you bought this book, you are either thinking about playing craps or are already a craps player, and in either case you want to be the best player you can possibly be. Well, if so, stick with the three basic bets I've taught you. Forget the rest.

HEAT!

The great dice hands in history used to be measured by how many passes the shooter made. A more common description now is how long the shooter held the dice. A shoot of ten or so passes is considered outstanding. Holding the dice for 20 or more minutes is fantastic!

I'll always remember the response when I asked a pit boss if he ever saw a player hold the dice for more than an hour.

"An hour?"

"Yeah, barring some ungodly slow table," I said.

"I've seen it about as often as a keno player hitting 12 out of 12."

"Twelve out of 12? I don't think anyone's ever done that, have they?"

"Right."

It's hard to separate fact from fiction when it comes to hearing tales about incredible dice hands. I can assure you that most of what you've heard are fish stories.

In all casinos worldwide, there are only a dozen or so confirmed reports per year of a dice hand lasting over one hour. A couple of years ago, three out of those delectable dozen occurred in Lake Tahoe (must be something in the water), but all of this is not to say it didn't really happen to your buddy at the office who just spent the better part of an hour detailing this great shoot in Vegas while he was out there on vacation. Maybe it did happen. Probably didn't. Otherwise, why is he still behind the desk? A shoot anywhere near an hour is what fortunes are made of. And I mean fortunes in the high six figures.

Besides, what's more important is the quality of the hand. Was it 20 minutes at a jammed-up table slowed up with players making prop bets and players arguing with the dealers, and shooters playing around with the dice, or was it a fast table with only a few players, and deft dealers working overtime? And what kind of numbers are we talking about here? Are we talking point numbers or are we talking craps, commonly referred to as **junk numbers**? Are the point numbers mostly 6s and 8s, or are we talking 4s and 10s? These differences, over 20 minutes or so, can be measured in the tens of thousands of dollars.

The most important item, however, is how you respond to such an event. It's like a dice dealer told me years ago: "Most players don't bet enough during a hot streak." I call it an opportunity missed.

A later chapter details the way I bet when I play craps. I follow a betting strategy I developed many years ago that I call Power Betting. The strategy helps to ensure that you don't miss out on that rare opportunity.

SITTING DUCKS

For most players, most of the time, it would seem as if the casinos are always at their best with the unfailing percentages on their side. Well, that's not exactly true. Otherwise, what's the point of playing? The casinos are not always at their best, and the unfailing percentages are not always unfailing. Maybe it just seems that way.

Years ago, a shift boss of a big Strip casino greeted me in the dice pit with this startling announcement: "John! You really picked a good time to come out here! We've been getting beat up badly at the dice tables! Come over here."

With his hand on my shoulder gently nudging me away from the action, we walk to an empty blackjack table where he spreads a file of papers that most players would never be privy to. A printout of the casinos' drop percentages over the past three weeks was a shocker. Turns out that the dice tables at this Fort Knox of all casinos actually had a break-in. Well, sort of. The dice tables over the past three weeks had lost money! Tons of money. Consistently. Continuously. The reports were all the evidence one would need to convict!

"Here, look at these figures. You won't believe it!"

Not only was there a negative sign in front of the drop at the dice tables, but it was the same story at the baccarat tables, too. The casino was losing big.

Just as hot and cold runs are common for the player in very short-term occurrences, such as hours or even days, so they are for the casinos, too, but in weeks, apparently, and maybe even a full month, if a player could be so lucky.

Since I just got in town, I had no chance to enjoy the first three weeks of duck hunting in the casino's shooting arcade. The dice tables were set up like a row of sitting ducks, and the shooters were using guns that actually shot straight. Give me a gun!

I'll tell you how I did. Pretty well, actually, but the tide was turning. During the first two days, I was bagging my limit, taking all the ducks that paraded in front of me. But by the third day, things were beginning to right themselves. The gun no longer shot straight, and someone had turned up the speed. Those ducks were zooming right on by.

The game was back to normal. The casino was breathing a little easier. And the only ducks flying over were hard 4s that never flew back.

DROP PERCENTAGES

The drop percentage should not be confused with the house percentage of each game. The drop percentage represents that portion of the players' money that the casino will win because of the house percentage. It's more correctly a measure of the amount of the players' original stake that the players will ultimately part with. In spite of all the different house percentages for each game, casinos generally earn from 17 percent to 20 percent in drop percentages for all the table games.

The term drop comes from the dealer's act of "dropping" the player's money through a slot on the table when exchanging cash (or markers) for chips.

Actual to-the-penny revenue per table cannot be tabulated as it can be for a slot machine where each bet and each payout is recorded by computer. If nothing else, the movement of chips from table to table prevents such accurate accounting for table games.

AMMO

What do you suppose we would find if we looked in the typical dice player's arsenal? For one, and perhaps for all, we would find only luck. But I would hope you already know how much good that is. No good! A round of luck is a round of blanks.

For another, we might find a liberal sprinkling of discipline. And that's very good. We might even find a shot of aggression. Good aggression. That's an assault weapon to blow down the limits. I don't think anyone can win without it.

For some, there's the skill of manipulating the dice. That's a howitzer that fires casino-piercing bullets. Casinos find it very difficult to defend against such an attack. And the casualties could run into the millions.

The ammo in my bag is perhaps a little different from most. I carry the right attitudes and the right disciplines. And I have plenty of patience. I know the game; I know the right bets to make. And now you do, too.

There's also the matter of stake money. I make sure my stake is sufficient. A few dollars doesn't work. A short stake usually means a short trip.

I don't carry the howitzer because the casino sees it as an illegal weapon (maybe the NRA should get in on this). The gaming industry has always had a tough time distinguishing between skill and scam. Ask any good card counter. The player's argument against such actions is that anytime someone is good enough to come up with a way to beat the casino, it's considered a scam, not a skill.

The casino wants you to rely only on luck; that's why they win. Luck won't beat the percentages. The casinos know that all too well. Tell them you want to play because you're feeling lucky, and they'll send a limo for you.

3 BEYOND THE BASICS

MY THINKING

Years ago, I enjoyed playing in tournaments, both craps and blackjack. During the '80s, table-game tournaments were a popular draw among the major casinos, particularly in Vegas. Now, the tournament scene has basically been relegated to slots. There are slot tournaments every time you turn around.

What hurt the table game tournaments in years past and what contributed to their near demise, was the fact that they became nothing more than a marketing tool for casinos. They were mostly run by the casino's sales and marketing people. It didn't take a marketing guru to figure out that slot tournaments drew more participants.

The concept of table-game tournament play was a good one, a very good one, and I enjoyed it very much. Particularly because a skilled blackjack player had to learn a new skill—tournament blackjack. Those who didn't bother to learn the ins and outs of playing in a tournament usually didn't fare so well. Skilled players who made critical adjustments to their game plan usually reaped the rewards.

In all my tournament play, I acquired a psychological perspective of gambling that became quite valuable to me for regular play. I began to treat each trip to the tables—each session—as a tournament of sorts, a tournament that I either

won or lost. Whatever I walked away with was the prize, winner take all. I didn't have to share it with anyone.

QUITTING A WINNER

When I play today, I don't even have to psych myself into it, it's an automatic thought process that has helped me—no, forced me—to quit winners. It's what a friend of mine calls a mind trick, but whatever you call it, try it, it might help you, too. Believe me, it has had a most profound effect on the most important part of my gambling, the bottom line. I consider it the Number One attribute that explains my success at the tables.

If I see that I'm up $500 at a dice table that suddenly turns choppy, I walk. The picture I see in my mind is the final round of a small tournament, just me and few other players all fighting for $500. And I just won it. Give me the cash; forget the plaque or the cheap little trophy. Five hundred dollars will be just fine. To the cashier's cage I go and I'm "awarded" five hundred-dollar bills. There's no official presentation, but it's not important. I won the tournament. I got paid. I'm happy. It's that simple. And it works.

A psychologist I often play with has told me why this "mind game" works for me, and why it might work for others. When I program myself to believe that I'm in a tournament, I take on that extra desire to win the tournament. And with it, comes the extra satisfaction of winning it. I'm simply transferring this extra incentive, a feeling of sheer satisfaction to a non-tournament event. The end result is I walk away a winner with an arbitrary amount of winnings that has made me feel as if it's time to leave the table because the "tournament" is over. It has, in reality, provided me with an indirect route to the most successful conclusion of what is the most difficult thing for players to do—quit winners!

Sometimes I'll leave a table with a mere $50 of profit in my hands. Okay, so it was a really small tournament, but I won it. It's time to get my cash prize, a crisp fifty-dollar bill.

You'll quickly see that the amount of the winnings is not the significant factor. It's the quitting winners that's significant. So I play in some big tournaments and I play in some little tournaments. My goal is to win the tournaments.

Savvy?

My psychologist friend is probably right in his assessment of why my mind trick works. I can remember many tournaments I played in where noteworthy players entered, too. Being naturally competitive, I would often compare my results with these particular players to see who finished higher. I wanted to win the tournament, of course, but I also wanted to beat them. There is a real drive to win in some of us that does go beyond the mercenary aspects of money. I believe it's important that we hone this drive to a fine edge. In the most elementary of terms, it's called a desire to win.

So, you ask, what if I were playing and during the course of the session I never was able to show a profit? What if there was never a time when I was up, even by fifty bucks, to realize my win and leave the table? Well, I can't win every tournament. I don't win every time I stand at a dice table. What's important during these sessions is that I realize a time when the tournament is over. I quit. I quit losers. Something that's tougher to do than quitting winners.

In a nutshell, setting up my play as winner-take-all tournaments has helped me to do what I've always said is the most difficult thing for most gamblers to do: to quit.

Here's another spin on what we just covered. If you are never ahead, you'll just have to take the bitter pill and quit losers. But when you are fortunate enough to be able to quit

winners, you must do it because if you don't, there's only one other option left: quitting losers, with that same bitter pill in your mouth.

If you are never ahead, you have no choice in what to do. But if you are ever ahead, you do have a choice: You can leave with chips in your pocket or you can leave with that pill you can't swallow. I like to think of the pill as your punishment for making the wrong choice.

STAYING POWER

If you recall from the first chapter, I mentioned that craps is the hunt for the hot hand. Players are on a safari. It's what makes craps so different from all the other casino games. But you need to pack a sufficient stake to last the trip. I've seen too many players who are plainly undercapitalized, so they either fall short in their hunt, or they change their game plan to make what little ammo they have stretch a little longer. And it just doesn't work.

The classic way that inexperienced players try to stretch their stake is by skipping, or chintzing, on the odds bets. It's a "scared money" scenario that plays out the same every time. If your stake is not large enough to make odds bets, then you must bring down the size of your wagers. If the casino's table minimums are too big for you, then find another casino.

Another way I see players trying to build up a short stack of chips is by ignoring the percentages and making what are called prop bets, such as hardways and elevens. Players are enticed by the supersized payoffs associated with these bets. As is most often the case with all casino games, however, bets that have a big payoff almost always have a high percentage. They don't have to. It's just that casinos have always believed they can hide these hefty percentages in the high payouts.

At the dice tables, **yo** means 11. And when you throw a yo to the dealer, you'll win on average one time out of 18 tries. But the house only pays you 15 to 1, instead of 17 to 1, for a supersized profit of over 11 percent. That's more than twice the edge against you at the roulette wheel, one of the casino's most notorious moneymakers. Remember that a bet on 11 costs you 11. Percentages like this will knock you out of a game faster than you can say "Yo-o-o-leven!"

If you absolutely must play with a limited stake, I can only hope you have the luxury of being able to play in competitive markets, such as Reno or Las Vegas, where table minimums are low and triple odds, or more, are offered. A dollar table is great. A dollar table with triple odds is even better. What you are most likely to find outside of Nevada, however, are $5 and $10 minimums.

At those levels, with a short stake, conservative betting is the order of the day. But I don't want to kid you into believing you can make it work. You might. But all you're doing is making a tough game even tougher to beat.

$20 BILL

I have a supplier in the book business who works harder than anyone I know. He's small, but he puts every effort into his product. And it shows. The last deal Bill and I did together was for a small embossing die that cost all of $200. When you consider all the phone calls, all the paperwork, and all the print revisions we made to tweak this thing, I doubt that his profit on the job was much more than a twenty-dollar bill. But that's the nature of his business. He works hard for a small profit.

So off we go for another weekend in Atlantic City. Bill loves to gamble. And that's an understatement. Gambling is his release valve from the pace of his hectic business. You don't know how many times he's twisted my arm to meet him out there. He always starts his play with a twenty on the table.

Money plays," he says, as he reels off a bill from his thick roll. He may need another, maybe two twenties next time. Maybe he can build up enough chip payoffs to keep his roll safely in his pocket. But not usually.

Whenever I see him lose a twenty-dollar bill on the tables, I can't help but think of all the work he goes through to earn one of those things. I don't know how many twenty-dollar bills he blows through in two days of nonstop craps, but I do know he has to make a lot of embossing dies when he gets back just to cover his losses.

Bill is the classic twenty-dollar bettor. He spends the bills like pennies in his pocket. Until he gets back home. Then, he treats them with a little more respect.

I hope you are a good respecter of money. Particularly when you're at the tables. But it's nice to respect money all the time. And it's not really the money per se that's worth your respect, it's the time and work that goes into earning it. If you work hard for your money, let go of it hard, too.

If it just so happens that it's easy for you to earn, and you have plenty of it, then show your respect from the standpoint of those who don't.

CONFIDENCE

Perhaps the most important quality you need in the casino is confidence. I'm sure all of you have heard the expression, "Winning instills confidence." But isn't this another one of those chicken-or-egg disputes? After all, if you are not adept at winning, if you don't win often, if you don't consider yourself a winner, honestly, then how can you have any confidence? How can you have any confidence in yourself at all?

And isn't it accurate to say that if you don't have confidence, then you can't be a winner? Barring a sprinkling of luck from time to time—that occasional fluke that lures you into a false sense of competency—don't you feel a coldness around you, an emptiness, because you have no confidence? Doesn't it feel like the forerunner of losing? Indeed. Sending luck to the sidelines for a moment, that luck of the draw that always catches you by surprise and keeps you in the game, isn't it pretty darn accurate to say that if you have little confidence in yourself and in your ability you probably won't win?

Well, here's what I believe. I believe that confidence must come first. I'm not even sure that winning is the best thing to instill confidence. Because if it were, in most cases, you would be relying on capricious luck to build your foundation of confidence. And I imagine it would crumble the next time you test it. In other cases, winning can instill overconfidence. I've always believed that being overconfident is just as harmful as having no confidence at all. When you arrogantly believe you are undefeatable, you are defeated.

The real confidence you need is simply instilled from your ability and your knowledge. Confidence builds gradually as you become capable of doing more things, as you learn more things, and as you experience these things over and over. But don't kid yourself. You can't force confidence if you only pretend you have the skills and the knowledge to be successful. Be true to yourself. If you don't think you have the ability and the knowledge, confidence will be a useless pretender, too.

And even if you have these traits, the confidence will still be lacking if you also know that you might not have the discipline to do what you know is right, to follow through on your plan, to patiently wait for the right opportunity, and to strike when the opportunity presents itself.

You need all these things to be a winner.

And if you really understand what I'm telling you, you'll also realize that you don't always have to win to be that winner.

THE PLAN

Everyone needs a plan to follow before even entertaining the notion of gambling. Part of that plan is a set of betting disciplines that can easily be incorporated into a betting strategy. One of the most powerful, Power Betting, is detailed in a later chapter. But there's more to having a plan than that. And the best way for me to convince you that you need a plan of action is to tell you a little story about a friend of mine who didn't believe in plans.

Lynn called me the other day and said he wanted to meet me in Atlantic City in September. I said, "Lynn, you just got back. Why do you want to go out there again?"

"I left ten grand out there, John, and it's gnawing at me. I gotta go out there and get it back."

"Well, what happened?" I asked, sensing his desperation. Desperation is the worst state of mind for a gambler.

"I was down five thousand going into Saturday morning. I had five hours to play before my ride to the airport. That lousy drive to Philly, you know?"

"Yeah. And I can imagine you pushed out some big bets, right?"

"Yeah. One bet. I put two thousand on the line and three thousand behind it. That's all I had left, John. It was all or nothing. The point was 10, I wanted the 10. I wanted a tough number. If it hit, I'd be up three thousand with the extra odds. The shooter was throwing so many other numbers, it looked promising, so I fished around in my pocket for some more chips, found two greens, fifty in cash, and I put it all on the hard 10 to bring it out. You know."

"So what happened? As if I don't already know."

"The damn dice came down the table with a 5-spot showing—I had half of it—and the other one spinning like a top. I mean, it just sat there and spun for what seemed like an eternity. I needed that other 5, John. But it slowed down and looked me in the eye with two spots. Right there in front of my face. I couldn't believe it."

"All or nothing, huh, Lynn? So how did you get home with no money?"

"I told the limo driver I'd mail him a nice tip. And I will. But I couldn't even get one of those Philly sandwiches at the airport. Had to pass it by. Couldn't even get a newspaper to read on the plane."

I told Lynn that for me to go out there with him, we would have to go out there with a plan. A conservative plan, not some screwy all-or-nothing shot that he's famous for. The plan, I told him, would have to be carefully designed to get his money back in stages, and his starting wagers would have to follow my Power Betting minimums. He balked at it. He knew Power Betting. I had taught it to him years ago. I might as well have taught it to a fence post.

"No way, John. That's too slow. How am I going to get back ten big ones with $15 bets?"

"They start at $15, Lynn, and you get up to greens early if the shoot is decent. It's for protection, Lynn, in case the dice don't cooperate. You're familiar with that, aren't you, Lynn? Lynn, we do this in stages, or go on your own."

"Okay, okay, John. But let me start in the middle of your strategy. I don't mind it so much if I can at least start with a quarter. Okay?"

"I suppose, Lynn, but you stick to it, and you stick to it every time."

We flew out together and spent the time on the plane working out a plan that included where we would play, when

we would play, and most important, when we would *not* play. We set tight loss limits, and minimum break times to regroup if we had to. We agreed we would only watch tables at first, to see if there was a drift to detect.

If I accomplished anything on that plane trip, at least I convinced Lynn that the fun was in the winning, not in the playing. Lynn liked to play. He likes to play a lot. And I told him that was one of his biggest problems. I finally got him psyched up to the point where he was looking for the win, not just looking for playtime.

The flight out there went fast; we were enjoying ourselves putting this plan together. Frankly, I don't think he had ever done this before.

We didn't play the day we arrived, as planned. We got to the hotel late in the afternoon and just strolled the boardwalk. We met a couple of friends for dinner and then retired early. We both like morning play, so we were up early the next day.

I won't bore you with our play-by-play, because most of the time we were walking away from the tables with $500, maybe $700 wins. But they added up. And Lynn was beginning to see that the right way to play was in planned sessions. He had learned how to walk away from a table a winner. Maybe not the big winner he was hoping for, but a winner, nonetheless. And he quickly realized how wins can add up.

We played 17 sessions. We know because we kept a diary of our play. Lynn liked the concept of keeping records so much that he even redesigned my form. (It's shown here and you are welcome to make a copy of it for your own personal use.)

PLAYER'S JOURNAL					
DATE	PLACE	STAKE	WALK	NET WIN	NET LOSS

Each line represents one session. **Stake** is the amount with which you begin a session. **Walk** is the amount you have at the end of a session. If you lost your stake, enter 0 under Walk (your Net Loss is your stake amount). If your Stake was $100, and your Walk was $250, enter $150 under Net Win. If your Walk was $75, enter $25 under Net Loss.

Lynn, incidentally, is a retired CPA, who sold his business and got a ton of money for it. That's his excuse for his big play and his big losses. Having the money is certainly no excuse for risking it. At the rate he was going, and without the accounting of his losses, he was playing blindly without even knowing how he stood. I think he simply didn't want to know.

I'll make a long story short. Lynn won $7,000. And at a time when he would have tried his famous "jump in and see if there are any rocks in the water" approach, he didn't do it. He didn't want to do it. He was happy that he had made a big dent in his previous beating. But what he was most happy about, though, was that he planned, and planned well, like the Lynn I used to know. Cautiously, conservatively at first, aggressively only when he saw opportunity. He played well. And he liked the way he played. He was proud of himself. To Lynn, that was worth much more than the winnings in his pocket.

Lynn came home a real winner.

RECORD KEEPING

Gamblers are generally poor record keepers. But there is so much you can learn from simple record keeping that I want to make it as easy as possible for you to do. Which is why I've reprinted the "Player's Journal" form for you. This simple accounting sheet helped my gambling friend immeasurably. It can help you, too.

Carry my book with you as you play and, after each session, make an entry noting the results of that session. Get into the habit of writing comments in the margins for each entry. Such things as the table minimum, how well you played, or any other significant thing worth noting for that particular session. Devise your own set of codes so you won't have to write a lot of stuff in such a small space. Now before you decide to chuck this whole idea (I'm reading your mind), let me tell you about one of my own learning experiences several years ago from using and studying my own journal.

In years past, I played at both $5 and $25 games. If the $5 tables were full, I didn't hesitate to play at a $25 table where there was almost always plenty of room to play.

One day, I looked over my journal and noticed an unusual recurrence. I quickly realized that my play at $25 tables generally showed a greater number of net wins than at the $5 tables! One might have expected the opposite, but my record keeping proved otherwise. I found this absolutely intriguing and had to find out why that was happening.

It turned out that the answer was a simple one. Whenever I would play at a $25 table, I would play much more conservatively. Most players would. I realized that I was tossing around red chips at a $5 table like they were, well, red chips, not green chips. I guess I didn't toss green chips around the same way because I had more respect for the higher value. I was simply more disciplined in my play with the greenies, more careful about making each bet.

The improvement in my play at the $25 table is the reason I fared better. It had nothing to do with the game percentages or the larger bets, and it had everything to do with my own cautious nature. Indeed. Caution at a dice table is a precious commodity.

Now, when I'm playing at a $5 table, I pretend the chips are green, not red. I treat the red chips with the same respect as I do the green chips. If you typically play with green chips, treat them as if they are black chips. You'll soon realize a remarkable difference in the quality of your play.

So, are you convinced now to keep records? In the hope that you are, the pages at the end of this book might turn out to be the most important pages of all!

TO PLAY OR TO WIN

Let's say you're out on a gambling trip, and decide to call home to tell your worrying wife how you did for the first day. "Don't worry, honey, I'm fine. I'm only down twenty bucks. I was up $200 at one point, but losing a little ol' twenty isn't too bad, is it honey, honey snookems?"

"You were up $200. Is that what you're telling me? And you ended up losing $20? What are you, some kind of jerk?"

"Now listen, honey…"

"No! You listen. You get that $200 back or don't bother coming home!"

There are two problems here. Two mistakes. For one, this guy obviously hasn't been married very long. He hasn't learned the routine, has he? Second, it's clear to me that this guy went off to play. Not to win. If he went on his trip to win, he would have quit with his $200 win. But no, he wanted to play. And play he did. He played his way through the $200 win and right into his $20 stake. He didn't lose $20. He lost $220.

You just can't sneak that by your wife.

You shouldn't even try to sneak it by yourself.

COMPLEMENTARIES

In *What Casinos Don't Want You to Know*, I devoted an entire chapter to comps, this interesting casino ploy that has reaped big rewards—for the casino. Table comps are my primary concern. Slot comps aren't so bad, generally speaking, as long as slot players play the way they would have played anyhow, without the lure of all the freebies.

To earn table comps, however, the key requirements are:

1. You start with big bets—the bigger the bets the bigger the comps.

2. You play for relatively long sessions. The longer you play, the better your comps.

This is precisely the reason why I have no interest in comps. The casino is playing its own little mind game with me. The casino is trying to control the way I play.

Well, I won't let that happen. I don't want to begin my sessions with big bets. I begin with small bets and proceed to larger bets only if I'm winning. And I don't intentionally play in long sessions. I like to hit and run. I purposely keep my sessions short. If I'm up a little, and I'm comfortable with my win, I'm history.

A friend of mine has a stock answer to why this and so many other aspects of gambling are true: If the casino wants you to do it, you shouldn't do it.

See if any of the following rings a bell:

- Mostly $10 minimums have been posted at the dice tables; you want to play at a $5 table but they're all busy. So you drift back to a $10 table and play anyhow.
- The casino has rows and rows of dollar slots; you want quarter machines. You can't find any that aren't being played because there aren't very many in the first place! So, you venture over to the dollar slots and play but you're just not comfortable.
- You hear the dice crew hawking high-percentage prop bets; you're tempted to make a few. You know better. But you watch while other players are getting paid and the dealers are saying, "Who else? Who else wants a piece of the hard 6?" You don't, but you throw ten bucks anyhow.
- The casino's cage has only two windows open and long lines have formed; you want to cash in your chips but you don't want to stand in line. So, you decide to go

back to the tables and play off the chips. Guess what? Well, at least now you don't have to stand in line.

You did exactly what the casino wanted you to do. The casino has its best interests—not yours—at heart. Don't let the casino control your play.

EXPERTISE

Let me close this chapter by taking you a little further out beyond the basics, where you'll be able to get a better perspective on gambling. It's a spot where few players have stood. As you learn to play craps, or any other casino game for that matter, I urge you not to get to the point where you consider yourself an expert. I'm not even sure if there is such a person. If there is, you'll most likely find them standing behind the tables, that is, casino bosses who have witnessed the games for decades on end. They've seen it all. They know what it's all about.

I've always believed these guardians of the games are the real experts in the casinos. Not the computer wizards and preppy whiz kids who know all the blackjack expected values and keno computations by heart.

When you see an "expert" gambler on television hawking his tapes, his books, his systems, or his Monday night NFL picks, you might want to think twice before you reach for your credit card. If the pitch is for instant riches, put the card back in your wallet and go buy a lottery ticket. You have about the same chance.

I did a QVC program recently where I spent the better part of eight minutes telling a national television audience of people who just love to buy things that the gambling books I publish are straight shooters—they tell it like it is. No hype, no empty promises, no impossible guarantees. That's right. No instant riches.

We sold 6,000 books in those eight minutes, so apparently there are players out there who are looking for an honest explanation of the games and want nothing less than realistic expectations. Indeed, maybe it was this difference that made the difference.

But there are also those players out there who are ready to buy the secrets of life. You can sell them anything. They are the market for the hustlers, and some would say they deserve what they get. To those of you who fall into that group, I say to you: Beware of false 'profits.' Beware of those who go over the line.

WIN $250,000 a Year Playing Craps!
You won't.

You Can Win Anytime in Any Casino!
You can't.

Monday Night NFL Winner Absolutely Free!
He's guessing just like you do.

I'm Retired and Living in Vegas on $200 Per Day Playing Blackjack! You Can, Too!
You'll be back at your old job in two weeks.

How to Find the Slot Machines That Are Ready to Pay!
Houdini couldn't find them.

It's not unusual for players, particularly rank beginners, to confuse expert sports figures with self-professed "expert" gamblers. In my own case, I consider myself a good player, but I lose many more times than you might expect. Any comparison to an expert tennis player or expert golfer is an absolute farce. On the tennis courts and on the fairways, expertise is a critical element woven throughout every single aspect of those games. The pro tennis player and the pro golfer, unlike the pro

47

blackjack players you hear about, use their expertise to put food on the table—and in most cases, money in the bank. No one would argue that expertise in sports pays off.

Expertise in sports means that the player has control over the game. But expertise in the casino, lawful expertise, that is, does not result in control over the game. An "expert" blackjack player, for example, cannot control the cards coming out of the shoe. An "expert" craps shooter cannot, or should not, have any effect on the roll of the dice. Even "expert" sports bettors cannot go down on the field and throw the football. They have absolutely no control over the contest. Sadly though, even that example needs to be clarified—they are not supposed to.

The only comparison we can make between games of sport and games of chance is that they are just that—games. For the average player going up against a top golf or tennis pro, there would be no match. And even that's not a fair comparison. Even top pros might have an off day. The casinos, however, are almost always at their best with solid percentages on their side of the tables. Expertise won't beat the percentages.

What's the matter? Am I painting the picture a little too bleak for you? What I'm doing for you is showing you true colors. That's the way I would want someone to do it for me. Spare me the hype and all the crazy promises that we've all heard before. If you're foolish enough to believe what your friend told you, or what you read in that little ad in the newspaper, you have some serious growing up to do.

The file of claims and guarantees I've collected over the years reminds me of the enticement ads we've all seen to enlarge a woman's bust size. It's a strange little contraption that you hold in your hand and squeeze for an hour or so each day. Within a few weeks—presto!—your bust miraculously grows from a flat 32 to a Dolly Parton size, whatever that is. I know all about this thing because my wife bought one. She's still a 32, but her hands are now stronger than mine!

And with all the states running lotteries, there's a new market for these charlatans. Lucky Numbers! Can you believe it? Thousands of people from all over the country, from all walks of life, send in money for their own personal lucky number.

What makes so many of us fall victim to these empty claims? It is, of course, the way we distort our dreams. We're looking for a shortcut to expertise. Actually, we don't really want to be experts. We just want someone to give us the winning numbers. We want it the easy way. Greed has a way of making us sour on our own dreams. Dreams that only come true the hard way.

I know one guy who makes the most unusual plans before he goes on a gambling trip. He starts thinking about whether or not all the pockets in his sport coat can accommodate all the envelopes he's expecting to bring home full of hundred-dollar bills. He starts thinking again about how he's going to hide all that loot from the IRS. Before the trip, he stops at his jeweler to make sure that Rolex he wants is still in the display case. "Hold it for me," he says for the umpteenth time. He doesn't want to just buy it, he wants to win it. He's so enamored with winning it, he doesn't realize that he could have owned one years ago spending just a fraction of his losses.

Gambling can do that to you. And it seems to hit about the time you start thinking that you might actually be an "expert" at all this. That's why I told you at the top of this piece that you really don't want to do that.

Gambling, my friend, is never the solution.

4 POWER BETTING

In *What Casinos Don't Want You to Know*, I revealed a betting strategy that I have used for decades. The reason it took so long to publish my strategy was simply a matter of not being able to make up my mind whether or not I wanted to tell my readers that I actually use a betting strategy. I was concerned that some readers might misconstrue my strategy as nothing more than a system. The term has picked up a rather tainted image over the years because of all the sucker systems that have been peddled to lure unsuspecting gamblers into a sinkhole. We touched on them briefly in the previous chapter.

Systems have one basic premise: to ensure, no, make that guarantee, a win! When I investigated systems in the mid '80s, I was amazed at what people would believe. And more amazed that they would spend hundreds, if not thousands, of dollars on worthless junk. This was snake oil medicine—arthritis, gout, and cancer cures—all over again. No one is cured. No one wins.

Those systems evolved from the larcenous minds of gambling shysters as a way to make an easy buck by duping players into believing they can overcome insurmountable odds and win consistently through some screwy method of playing craps or blackjack or roulette (roulette was a favorite game of these hucksters), or picking football games, or picking horses, or whatever your poison. In the parlance of the trade, it's called "giving the customer what the customer wants." It's true. Gamblers want to win so badly that they'll believe anything.

I remember one guy in particular who ran newspaper ads promising $500 a day playing a blackjack system. The scam was: He plays, you finance. And he gets to keep whatever he wins over the five hundred. If he loses, well, what does he care? It was your money! This crook has surfaced again, and now he's in a new trade. He's selling lucky lottery numbers. And people are buying!

If you didn't know it by now, you'll know it right now, because I'm going to tell you: No system ensures, much less guarantees, a win. Worthless. That's really all that systems ever were and ever will be. So now you can see why I hesitated. The betting strategy I published, called the Gollehon Betting Strategy, is not a system because the intent is not to ensure winning. I can't do that for you. No one can. Indeed, the intent of the strategy is to help protect you against three things:

1. Sudden losses out of the gate
2. Accumulative losses that tend to sneak up on you.
3. Equally important, your missing out on a big win because of a whimpering fear of building up bets as you continue to win.

The strategy restricts your betting levels at the outset, continuously controls the level of betting, sets limits on losses, yet forces betting levels to increase as wins increase.

That's its job. And it does it well. But unlike a system, it doesn't promise a Mercedes, a BMW, and a Lexus, all sittin' cozy in your 3-stall garage. You'll have to work hard for that stuff on your own.

SAFE HARBOR

I recently ran into a player to whom I had taught the strategy years ago. He was still using it! He told me that the strategy is his safe harbor. He said, "John, it's as if you're playing right beside me, telling me how to bet, what to do next. With your strategy, I never feel that I'm playing alone."

It humbles me to think that players feel so strongly about my strategy. And I particularly liked this guy's metaphoric safe harbor comparison because I feel the same kind of protection when I'm using it.

The Gollehon Betting Strategy not only tells you when it's time to open up the throttles, it also tells you when it's time to dock your boat and batten down the hatches. In all the years I've played my strategy, I've found myself in rough waters many times. There are more storms brewing in casinos than on the Weather Channel. But in all those years, I've never had to abandon ship.

MODIFIED STRATEGY

I mentioned in *What Casinos Don't Want You to Know* that I use a modified version of the Gollehon Betting Strategy for craps, and that brief mention generated considerable mail from dice aficionados. You see, the Gollehon Betting Strategy is best suited for games with singular, even-money bets, such as blackjack, baccarat, and certain roulette bets. It takes some doing to make it fit the way most dice players play—with multiple bets.

More than that, however, the strategy was said to be a bit too conservative for craps, even in the aggressive schedule. I don't know that I necessarily agree with that; I'm simply reporting the comments from my readers. It is true that my special strategy for craps, called Power Betting, which I am

about to reveal to you, is more aggressive, but I think you'll see as you read on that any lesser betting levels may not achieve the success we all want.

There is risk. There is always risk when you gamble. As is the case with my original strategy, I always recommend that all players begin with the conservative schedule. There are two schedules to choose from: conservative and aggressive. Later, if you believe your comfort level will not be compromised by higher betting amounts, then, and only then, should you consider the aggressive schedule. You must be totally comfortable with the strategy you will be using.

GAME ADVANTAGES

In all my years of casino gambling, I quickly realized that the dice tables offer a greater likelihood of large wins without large risk through judicious betting of streaks. The game even has its own built-in streak thanks to the 5 to 1 odds of a 7. You are not expected to lose your bet on any one roll, nor are you expected to win it. And what can happen during the interim is what gambling fortunes are made of.

If point numbers are parading, as the dice bosses like to call a long string of passes, the player's fortunes can run into the tens and even hundreds of thousands of dollars. I've seen wins at the dice tables that blow away wins at the blackjack tables—hands down!

What's really nice about this game is that you don't need to begin with relatively large bets. In fact, you shouldn't. Power Betting prevents you from doing just such a thing. Large betting at the outset is no precursor of a hot streak. Dice tables get hot when they feel like it. The trick is to be mentally and financially prepared to strike when the iron is hot. And that's what Power Betting is all about.

Unlike the Gollehon Betting Strategy, Power Betting offers a more aggressive attack in both the conservative and aggressive modes. For example, Power Betting's first level is the same for both conservative and aggressive bettors.

This modification was necessary to increase the aggressive behavior of the strategy in the early stages of a potentially long streak. Any additional risk at this early level will come back to you with exponential growth if the streak sustains itself into the third level. It's like investing in a fast-rising stock. Do you want to buy it when it's cheap, or buy it when it's overpriced?

THE 4 STRATEGY ADVANTAGES

1. Makes your betting at the dice tables virtually automatic. There are no tough decisions to make. Nothing to ponder. You simply let the strategy do the work!

2. Protects you out of the gate against sudden losses. Plus, you'll gain additional protection against gradual losses that could otherwise become substantial.

3. Ensures that you won't miss out on a big win. Power Betting gives you the fortitude to take full advantage of a hot streak.

4. Offers two different schedules of betting for either conservative or aggressive players.

THE POWER BETTING STRATEGY

CONSERVATIVE $5 / $10*	PRE-PLAY	AGGRESSIVE $15
25		25
50	Any loss in this FIRST level returns you to pre-play	50
75		**75**
100	REPEAT OPTION (see text)	100
150	Any loss in this SECOND level returns you to $25	200
200		**300**
300		500
400	Any loss in this THIRD level returns you to $75	1000
600		1500

*Two levels of pre-play. See text.
Follow the progression only after a point number win with double odds.
Generally, wins on the come out do not dictate an increase in bet level.

POWER BETTING OVERVIEW

Before we look at the rules for this exciting strategy, a brief overview of the way it works will help you understand the rules better and learn the strategy quicker.

Essentially, the strategy is broken down into two schedules: a "softer" betting schedule for conservative players, and a "stronger" schedule for aggressive players. As I mentioned earlier (it bears repeating), all players should begin with the conservative schedule. Later, if you believe your comfort level will not be compromised by higher betting amounts, then, and only then, should you consider the aggressive schedule. You must be totally comfortable with the strategy that you will be using.

Power Betting is only for pass line bets and come bets—the lowest percentage bets on the table. Other bets at the dice tables present the player with too high a percentage and cannot be recommended. Designing a powerful betting strategy for higher percentage bets seems almost sacrilegious. Now if it just so happens you like to make hardways and place bets and even field bets from time to time, don't sit there whining at me thinking about how much fun these bets are and how you can't bear to play craps without them. Believe this: The fun is in the winning. It is not in the playing.

Think about it. Then think about it some more. Winning is the name of the game.

The betting amounts listed in the strategy are the flat wagers that go on the pass line or on the come. The flat wager is always paid off at even money if it wins. If a point number is rolled on the come out, you must always back up your flat wager with double odds, which is paid off at true odds (the true likelihood of making the point number before making a 7). There is no house advantage to this bet! It is a fair bet. It is the only fair bet in the casino! If you are following the progression on your way to a nice win, and the next bet calls for a flat wager of $250, the odds bet will be $500! And you must do it! The odds bet is the key to the big win. Trust the strategy.

Your first bets are called **pre-play**. All early betting must follow the rules of pre-play, which basically hold you to a near table-minimum level until certain triggers occur that allow you to enter the progression. It's also possible, even likely, that other triggers will force you to exit the session to protect against early losses. Your exits will occur most often in pre-play, so you should not be alarmed that you are not riding the progression as often as you would like. We are all at the mercy of the laws of random numbers. Finding an anomaly in the laws may take time. Indeed, it takes patience to win. Generally speaking, if you do find yourself making early exits frequently, it simply means the table conditions were too risky to continue.

If, however, you are fortunate enough to survive pre-play and actually enter the progression, at no time do you continue with the schedule following a loss. A loss in the progression always sends you back down to a particular level for your next

bet (called a **drop-down bet**) as dictated by the rules. In most cases, you'll find that a loss in the progression sends you back to pre-play because most of your losses will be in the first level.

Many players, without benefit of Power Betting, might elect to continue the progression in the hope that the loss was just a glitch on their way to riches. Well, we don't want to rely on hope to get us through, we want to rely on the strength of Power Betting to get us there. Continuing the progression following a loss is a potentially huge mistake. The reason for this is quite simple: The first loss you will have experienced will have been your largest bet. Why risk an even larger bet that you might also lose? By doing so, you could effectively wipe out all the previous gain! Such reckless actions might even put you into the red. What a revolting development!

As we now go into the actual rules of Power Betting, promise me, and promise yourself, that you will follow the rules religiously.

POWER BETTING RULES

1. Take to the session a stake of $100 for the conservative strategy, or $200 for the aggressive strategy.
2. Enter the session with a pre-play pass line bet of $5 for the conservative strategy, or $15 for the aggressive strategy.
3. For the conservative strategy only:
   a. Increase your pre-play pass line bet to $10 when you are able to show a net win of $30.
   b. If the $10 bet wins, continue at this level as long as you continue winning and until one of the entry rules (listed below) is triggered. At that point you will enter the progression, but

you may only do so immediately following a winning $10 wager. You cannot jump to the progression from the $5 level.

   c. If any bet at this $10 level loses, return to the $5 level and follow rule 3(a) for returning to the $10 level.

4. Exit the session if you lose three out of four consecutive bets, or lose three bets in a row. (The author will often play this rule more stringently and actually exit a session after two consecutive losses. Your choice.)

5. Exit the session if your stake drops to $50 using the conservative strategy, or $100 using the aggressive strategy.

6. Enter the progression only after you accomplish one of the following in pre-play:
   a. Win three out of four consecutive bets
   b. Win three bets in a row
   c. Show a net win of $75

7. Increase your bet to the next amount in the progression as long as you win each bet. However, this rule applies only after a point number win with double odds. (With rare exception, wins on the come out while in the progression do not dictate an increase in bet level. See "Explanation of the Rules" that follows.)

8. Decrease your bet whenever you lose in the progression, as follows:
   a. If the loss occurs in the first level, return to your pre-play minimum.
   b. If the loss occurs in the second level, return to the start of the progression.
   c. If the loss occurs in the third level, return to $75, the last bet in the first level. This bet that

follows a loss in the progression is called a drop-down bet.

9. If the drop-down bet wins while in the progression, continue the progression from that point.

If the drop-down bet loses while in the progression, return to pre-play and follow rules 4 through 6 for exiting the session or re-entering the progression.

If the drop-down bet was made in pre-play, regardless of whether it wins or loses, stay in pre-play and follow rules 4 through 6 for exiting the session or re-entering the progression.

THE 9 RULES OF WINNING

First of all, it's important to note that all of the rules, with the exception of rule 3, apply to both the conservative and aggressive schedules.

Rule 1

Learn how to start each session with the same size stake. All good gamblers I know do this. It's a mark of discipline. Don't walk up to a dice table and fish around in your pockets for whatever you can scrounge up. Do you think that looks pro? Have a C-note handy and present it to the dealers for chips by dropping it on the table while saying, "Change 100." Personally, when I do this, I purposely lay the bill across part of the field and part of the come, or part of don't pass and part of the come. That way, in case I'm confronted with a deaf dealer, there's no question that my money doesn't play!

Conservative players might be concerned about starting out with $100. They shouldn't be. One hundred dollars is not a loss limit. On the contrary. Rule 5 limits the conservative player's loss to $50.

So, why not start out with $50 instead of $100? Because I also want you to learn how to leave a cold table with a goodly portion of your stake. It may only be psychological, since either way it's a $50 smack in the teeth, but I never want to put you in a position where you walk away with nothing. There's no worse feeling.

Incidentally, just because Rule 5 says you walk at $50, that doesn't mean you can't walk earlier. That's something else I don't want to do; I never want to come across as forcing a player to play to a certain limit, or for a certain length of time. Quit whenever you want to.

The next thing you do in this situation is go to the cage and exchange the remaining chips for cash. And, if you're like me, you'll record the session in your journal. Doing these things has a secondary purpose: It gives you something to do during your break from the tables. You might even want to get a cup of coffee and plan your next session.

> This is an important discipline to follow, so allow me to repeat it: Always cash in your chips when you exit a session. Never begin a session with chips. Always begin a session with cash.

If you have won a considerable amount of money from prior sessions, lock up your money, literally. Most casinos offer safety deposit boxes at no charge to you. Never carry large amounts of cash on your person.

Another advantage of using a safety deposit box is to keep you away from your winnings! I hate to see players risking more than just a small portion of their winnings for stake money.

Key question: So when do you go back and tackle the table again? Is five minutes too soon? You're darn right it is! Take a break. Relax. Eat lunch. Go for a walk. Check out some other tables. Check out the pool. Check out the action. At the tables, that is. What's the point of quitting a bad table if you're going to head right back?

Rule 2

Pre-play starts with five bucks on the line for the conservative player, or a whopping fifteen bucks for the aggressive player. I know some high rollers who will get quite a laugh at that. Fifteen bucks isn't even enough for their tip money. And $15 won't get these guys any comps, either. Too bad. This book is for players who want to win, not for players who want to impress.

Rule 2 is important, so let's get serious a moment. Remember that this rule is for openers, what I call **early betting**, and it's also to provide a safe harbor after an early collapse up the progression. Sure, pre-play bets are small, but they are supposed to be! When you do get to the progression, however, you'll run into some pretty big bets as you creep up. Trouble is, most high rollers like to start with the big bets. And guess what usually happens.

If some players were to see me playing craps at the very beginning of a session, they might be surprised—if not bored— watching me bet a thin nickel on the pass line with an even thinner dime behind. Five bucks on the line and ten bucks in odds is not going to pop many eyes. No jaws are going to drop.

But I'm not bored. And I really don't care what anyone else thinks about the way I play. I'm busy. I'm hunting. Like most players, I'm after the hot shoot that can send me up the progression. Unlike most players, however, I bide my time in getting there, if I get there. Either way, I enjoy the hunt.

Now if those same players were to see me again at that same table an hour or so later, it's possible I might be throwing black chips around like candy. I might have a couple of thousand in chips spread over the table with piles more in front of me!

If other players were to spot me at that very moment, they might actually confuse me with a high roller. That's what Power Betting can do for you.

Rule 3

The $5 and $10 dual-level betting is a special pre-play progression to help conservative bettors get in a safer position for a possible entry into the main progression. It's important that conservative bettors heed this rule to smooth out their entry into the progression when the conditions are appearing optimum. The rule also helps to extend their staying power to increase the likelihood of catching a hot hand. An additional advantage is the extremely conservative nature of the early betting to protect against sudden losses without significantly creating a late entry into the progression.

Rule 4

This exit rule protects against the possibility of getting beaten by negative streaks. We're looking for hot streaks, not cold streaks, so keep a keen eye on losses that seem to gang up on you. Why take the risk that these cold streaks will only continue?

If such cold streaks develop late within the first dozen hands, you'll most likely have more than one reason to exit the table. It's not unusual for both exit rules to trigger at the same time.

Personally, when such poor table conditions are encountered, I won't return to that table for the rest of the day. Period.

Rule 5

This critical exit rule is simply to guard against an indiscernible trend. Dice players call this condition **choppy**. What it really means is the game is beating you so slowly that you don't realize it. Stop the trend at $50 if you're using the conservative strategy, and at $100 if you're using the aggressive strategy.

Incidentally, don't be concerned that you are exiting tables too frequently as you apply Rules 4 and 5. You will definitely find that there are more times than you imagined when the

rules tell you to quit. And what you'll be doing is something you probably never did as often as you should have: restricting your losses!

Rule 6

Finally we get out of pre-play and start the progression! The conditions that trigger Rule 6 are all positive. Winning three out of four consecutive hands is definitely a good sign; winning three hands in a row is even better. Best, of course, is actually showing a decent net win of $75. What better time to start your assault?

The only exception to this rule is in pre-play of the conservative strategy where you can only enter the progression from the $10 level, regardless of what you accomplished at the $5 level. In this case, Rule 3 takes precedence over rule 6.

Rule 7

This is the fun part. Both the conservative and aggressive strategies start with $25. As long as you win, proceed to the next bet. However, such increases may only follow a point number win with double odds. Otherwise, you may find yourself beginning the progression at the $25 level, winning the bet on the come out with an 11, for example, and then being forced to bet $50 with the chance of having to back it up with $100 if a point number is established. I said this special strategy I use is aggressive, but not that aggressive!

However, if you are in the progression, say, at the $50 level, and win four bets in a row on the come out, you may feel comfortable proceeding on to the $75 level since you are now blessed with some nice winnings in your tray. But a loss at the $75 level if the bet goes with odds ($225 at risk) would wipe out your four wins at the previous level. My personal preferences have usually been to keep my bets static on the come outs, and let increases come only after a win with odds.

If you are so fortunate to have caught a streak that takes you through the first 3-bet level, you could be ahead to the tune of at least $750 depending on:

1. Which point numbers were bet (the odds payoffs vary, of course)
2. Whether the wins were come out wins or point number wins
3. The amount of your pre-play win

Both the conservative and aggressive players are presented with an interesting option if they make it through the first level. The first bet of the second level is $100, and it may be repeated before progressing. The progression changes in value from that point on between the two difference schedules. The $100 bet is a key bet in order to maintain a nice win to that point. Both the $75 bet in the first level and the $100 bet beginning the second level are **hurdle bets**. You need to get over at least one of these hurdles to retain a decent win following your eventual loss.

Accordingly, I always recommend using the repeat option as a safeguard to preserving a goodly portion of your winnings.

As you can appreciate, most of the time the progression takes you only into the first level. But do yourself a big favor. Take it as far as the consecutive wins will go. Don't be nervous. Enjoy the ride up!

Rule 8

Yes. All good things do come to an end, sometime. This rule protects you from doing something stupid like continuing the progression after a loss.

There's an old gambler's maxim that certainly applies here: Never press a loss. The term **press** means to double the amount of your previous wager in the hope of both winning the bet and making up for the loss.

Indeed, the right move is to reduce your bet with a drop-down wager, and that's what Rule 8 tells you to do: Your next bet following a loss in the progression is reduced in proportion to the size of your losing wager.

Some players elect to exit the table after a losing bet that ended a lengthy progression. Let's say they were at $100 when they lost the bet. They can't bring themselves to cut back, so they quit. Well, quitting is far superior to continuing the progression, but the smarter choice is to follow Rule 8 and simply cut back. With all the success you've just had, it's possible the loss was just a blip in your future, and you may be headed back up again.

Rule 9

This interesting rule covers all scenarios following a drop-down bet. If you lose the drop-down wager, that means you lost two bets in a row and you are relegated to pre-play again. If you were only in the first level when you experienced your first loss, your drop-down wager was already in pre-play. Follow Rules 4, 5, and 6 for exiting the session or re-entering the progression.

If you win the drop-down bet while in the progression, continue with the progression at the next amount directly higher than the drop-down bet. For example, if your first loss in the aggressive progression was $300 (in the second level), your drop-down bet will be $25. If you win that bet, your next wager will be $50.

There's nothing that says you can't quit instead of returning to pre-play or making a drop-down bet. If you want to quit, quit! In fact, quit any time you want to, although I can't understand why anyone would want to quit while riding a nice win streak. Most often, if players elect to quit on their own (not being forced to quit by rule), it's usually at that moment when they otherwise would have been relegated to pre-play.

But if you do feel like playing some more, follow the pre-play rules and see if you can re-enter the progression. If pre-play doesn't work out and you're forced to exit the session, go outside and get some fresh air. It's probably time for a break, anyhow.

MULTIPLE BET RULES

It is difficult to make hard-and-fast rules regarding multiple bets. Experienced players know that their decision to increase the number of bets often hinges on a host of factors, not the least of which is their standing at that particular time. Are they up, are they down, are they even? What's the drift of the table? Choppy, little cold, little warm? If it's clearly cold, or clearly hot, the decision is obvious. It's just that most of the time it's something else, and the decisions are hard to make.

In many cases, my own decisions as to how many bets I have out are usually made from my gut, not from my heart, and not even from my head. It's a personal matter to me, but I've shared it before; I have no qualms sharing it again. I trust in my instincts. If I have a strong indication—and don't ask me to explain it—that a particular shooter is about to kick up a storm, you might see me load up the come right out of the gate. Two or three come bets working early is not unusual for me. But only if I feel very very good about it.

Hopefully, you'll understand the problem I have giving you hard-and-fast rules about multiple bets. But at least there are only four:

1. Start your session with just a pre-play bet on the pass line.
2. Increase your number of bets as a function of your winnings.

3. Each multiple bet is subject to the Power Betting Rules and is completely independent of each other.

4. Note carefully how each bet performs so that you can follow Power Betting Rules 4, 5, and 6 for exiting the session (quitting that particular bet) or entering the progression.

MORE ON MULTIPLE BET RULES

Rule 1

There are obvious exceptions to this rule. If the table heats up just about the time you start the session, you'll have to make a judicious decision as to how many come bets you'll want to risk. Why not try one, and if it wins, try two?

Rule 2

There is no better way to gauge the increase in the number of bets. Power Betting determines the size of your bets. So let your winnings—or losses—determine how many.

The more you're winning, the more bets you can make. If you're not winning—let's say you're just barely holding your own—one come bet is plenty.

Rule 3

The only time chips relating to multiple bets are counted together is for the sake of Power betting Rule 5. This important exit rule applies to all of your chips, including those on the table.

The more bets you are making, the more likely that Power betting Rule 5 will impact on you. Remember that a pass line bet in $5 pre-play and a couple of come bets built the same way means you have $45 at risk. The roll of a 7 would claim nearly half of your stake.

Rule 4

If a come bet loses early, and another loses, and yet another, it should be obvious that multiple bets are not working at that moment. Your decision is easy: Stick with just the pass line bet, unless it isn't working, either.

Of course, you can have a situation where one come bet is well into the progression while your pass line bet, and even other come bets, are going nowhere.

That's the fun of craps. The streaks can happen on the pass line—six or seven straight passes are certainly not unusual—or they can happen in the come. It's not unusual for players to win several hundred dollars with a few come bets while their pass line bet sits as a lonely nickel on the line.

5 21 QUESTIONS & ANSWERS

Most observers believe that craps is the toughest game in the casino to bet. In consideration of all the players I've watched over the years, I can see why people think that way, and why they eventually shy away from the game. *Conquering Casino Craps* teaches you how to bet easily and sensibly. Forget the way other players bet. Other players only make it tough on themselves. And tough on their wallets.

Craps isn't any more tough to bet than it is tough to learn. But the game just seems to pull out more bets from the pockets of players who just don't know better. And maybe that's the real problem.

It's tempting to bet the hardways. It's tempting to make a spread of place bets. It's even tempting to some to make bets in the field. Surprisingly, all the bets that seem to confuse observers, and even players themselves, are bets that shouldn't be made in the first place! Like I said, craps just has a way of, well, tempting players into betting their ass off. I suppose the first rule of playing this game should be to avoid temptations.

Indeed, it's a game full of action that sometimes gets compared to Wall Street. Some of the similarities are interesting, but make no mistake. There is no comparison to legitimate investing. Spreading bets around a dice table is one thing; spreading your investments around is another. Asset Allocation does not work on a dice table.

Since playing the game is basically betting the game, I wanted to do an entire chapter on the most commonly asked questions about craps, which, not surprisingly, always seem to have something to do with betting. We've talked at great length about betting this game, but it's likely that you still have questions, particularly about Power Betting. Hopefully, they will be answered in the following pages.

QUESTION: Why is it that the dealers are always hawking the bets that you say are not worth making, like hardways and C&Es?

ANSWER: You wouldn't expect them to push the low-percentage bets, would you? They are doing what their bosses tell them to do. You'll find some of the finest casino hustles at the dice tables. It's a part of the presentation. Simply learn how to tune it out.

QUESTION: A dealer offered to help me learn craps and showed me how to make field bets. But my husband said the field bets are high percentage. If so, why did the dealer do this?

ANSWER: A brush-off, I would say. Many dealers are still from the old school; they think dice is a man's game, which is plainly absurd. These dealers tend to relegate women players to the easy bets like the field. It's upsetting to me, too. I wouldn't be surprised if the term male chauvinist pig originated at a dice table.

Please don't let this stop you from playing. Read my book. Learn the smart bets. Your husband, by the way, is right. Field bets are not smart bets.

You should know that casino managers finally have begun hiring women dealers for the dice tables, adding a much needed new dimension to the game.

Incidentally, don't ask players for guidance, either. All dice players think they're experts. And you know what an expert is, right? According to a Florida football coach, "An expert is a guy who sits on the 50, criticizes the coaches and the players, and has all the answers. Then, he leaves the stadium and can't find his car."

QUESTION: In Vegas, they've got a bet called the Big 6 and Big 8 on the corners of the layout. But I don't see them in Atlantic City casinos. Why?

ANSWER: These bets are sucker bets, since they pay even money on 6s and 8s that could earn 7 to 6 when made as a place bet. The Atlantic City Casino Control Commission does not allow the bet. Nevada should follow suit.

QUESTION: It seems to me it would be easier to keep my chips separated for each multiple bet I'm making. Do you do this?

ANSWER: Some players like to keep their stake separated into two or three piles of chips, each pile for each multiple wager. You can do this at first, if you like, but you'll soon find out that it really isn't necessary. In most cases, it just confuses things.

For example, the exit rules apply to your entire stake, not to any portion thereof. Having your stake separated may hide the fact that an exit rule has been triggered. Plus, it's likely you'll be at one bet, then two, then one bet again, then two, then maybe three, and back to one again. So, to keep separate accounting for each bet becomes an unnecessary chore.

You'd be surprised how easily you'll know what each bet is doing and how you are doing overall. Just looking at the size of the wagers should tell you whether or not any particular bet is working out.

The only chips you will want to separate, if you are able to, are your winnings from your original stake. This way, you will be able to track your winnings more easily. Incidentally, winnings (or remaining stake money) counted while a session is ongoing include those chips in action on the table.

QUESTION: I can't stand to begin a session with just a pass line bet. I like to put at least two or three come bets in action early. You said you do this, too. Right?

ANSWER: Not quite. I said I do this when I feel very, very good about the session. It's a gut call for me. What it isn't is an excuse to load up the table. It's my reaction to instinct. Frankly, I can't imagine anyone playing without using it. Although I said it is not unusual for me to do this, it is certainly not frequent. In other words, I have what I consider a valid reason for doing it; you don't.

If you have several bets on the table, all in pre-play, all early in the session, and a not particularly profitable session at that, I strongly question the sense of your actions. You are not giving pre-play a chance to do its job. Pre-play minimizes your exposure at the outset and whenever you are not winning.

Let's say you had two or three bets well into the progression that got knocked out with a 7, and you decide to put three new pre-play bets back on the table, hoping the next shooter can restore the thrill. You're breaching the rules, but at least you're doing it at a time when you would have substantial winnings in front of you. Nonetheless, I can only recommend that you go back to the single pass line wager in pre-play. If that doesn't excite you enough after stringing three successful bets on the progression, then the better choice is to leave the table and go cash in your hoard of chips. As time passes, the need for excitement diminishes, and the need for protection and common sense returns.

QUESTION: The problem I have with Power Betting is that it isn't designed for someone who makes place bets. I'm very successful with these bets. I like to cover all the numbers, sit back, and watch the dealer pay me.

ANSWER: You are worse than the eternal optimist; you come across to me as the eternal bonehead. First of all, the strategy does not apply to place bets because the percentages on those bets are too high. In other words, place bets are not worth devoting a strategy to. Granted, the 6 and 8 are a mere 1.52 percent, but that's nearly three times higher than the percentage on a pass line or come bet with double odds. Placing the 5 and 9 costs you 4 percent, and buying the 4 and 10, a better percentage than placing these numbers, will set you back nearly 5 percent.

Second, covering all the numbers is extremely risky. You realize, of course, that a 7 wipes out all of your bets. By making these bets, you are raising the odds of winning (making them worse). Reread the section in Chapter 1 about this rather common, often tempting, but obviously dangerous aspect of craps.

QUESTION: I don't like to make come bets because you have to make the number twice. I like place bets because you only have to make the number once.

ANSWER: Your logic isn't working. This complaint is far and away the most often heard around a craps table.

First of all, with a pass line bet or come bet, you don't have to make the number twice, because at the outset there is no specific number to make. Before the bet, do you know which number it is that you will have to make twice? Of course not. And once you make it, do you actually think there's less likelihood of making it again because you just made it the first time? The dice aren't keeping track. Can you imagine hearing the dice talking to themselves, saying, "Hey, we just came up 6, so that's enough for that number. Let's do an 8 next time."

Most players confuse the odds of making pass line or come bets with the odds of rolling a given number twice. For example, the odds of rolling a 4 before you roll a 7 are 2 to 1. The odds of rolling a 4 twice before rolling a 7 are 8 to 1. But if 4 just happens to be your point number on the pass line, nobody told you before you started that you had to make two 4s!

QUESTION: Let's say I have the 6 covered on the pass line, and the 8 and 9 covered on the come. Time and time again some shooter will make the 4 and the 5 and the 10, and then the 4 again, so I'm tempted to cover these numbers, too, with place bets, but then I have too much at risk. Any solution?

ANSWER: If the shooter isn't hitting your numbers, it isn't going to help to put more bets out. Those other numbers the shooter made are gone. If you do make more bets, you've accomplished exactly what you posed in your questions: You have put yourself at greater risk.

Your question reminds me of a guy who wrote to me years ago complaining about what he called, wasted numbers. He said he hated to see a shooter making numbers that he didn't have covered with come bets, so his solution to the problem was simply to cover the remaining numbers with place bets, just as you are proposing.

An earlier question addressed this similar concern, so it's probably fair to say that many players share it. But covering numbers with place bets is a costly way of winning. You'll win a few bets, but your losses will far exceed your winnings. It makes no sense to load up all the numbers with come bets, either, unless you are experiencing one very hot hand. To do this out of the gate, however, is particularly senseless for all the reasons we've talked about.

In case you are still not convinced, let me pose a simple question to you. Let's say you are going to play the state lottery. And, knowing how you don't like to see winning numbers wasted, would you consider buying all the numbers? It might be an extreme exaggeration, and not exactly a fair comparison, but the message should be clear.

The dice table is full of "if only" players—if only I had done this, if only I had done that. "If only" players are greedy players who want it all and want it now. What I believe, in contrast, is that you take what you can get. And be thankful. Trust me, players. The key to playing this game is "protection." And protection is the underlying strong point of Power Betting.

I'm sure you now realize why place bets are not included in the Power Betting Strategy. Besides the higher percentages against the player, they do tend to put players at greater risk because, as we've clearly noted, they tempt players into making more bets than they should.

Place bets, you see, are a quick way to get the numbers you want, instead of waiting for them to come to the number with smarter come bets. You can't force the numbers by betting the numbers. But try telling that to a place bettor.

Casinos know it. I know it. Now you know it. Place bettors are greedy!

QUESTION: What if the shooter is making a lot of numbers but not the point?

ANSWER: Sounds good to me! And it's a pretty good sign that you should make a come bet or two, in the hope of cashing in on a string of numbers being thrown. But as I said in my answer to the previous question, you have no assurance the shooter is going to continue the streak of numbers. It's a tough decision to make, and only you can make it.

Personally, I would launch two come bets into play and take it from there. Without reservation.

We just finished talking about what it feels like to see an array of numbers parade in front of you that you didn't have covered. When this happens to me, I don't cringe at the sight

of those nice numbers I don't have. I don't do the "if only" routine, and I don't stand around stewing about it because I know those numbers are history. I take it in stride, but I do react to it.

The way you react to it, however, is the crucial element of how you play the game. You absolutely must respond to it, but in moderation, by following the multiple bet rules.

QUESTION: In your book, *What Casinos Don't Want You to Know*, I enjoyed your story about a hot hand at the Las Vegas Hilton, and the premonitions you had about the session. But I'd like to know why, at a point well into the shoot, you converted your come bets to place bets on the 5, 6, 8, and 9, and buy bets on the 4 and 10 as you describe. This appears to be contrary to your statements that it is not smart to make place bets.

ANSWER: Tough question. Tough answer.

That incredible session was many years ago, and the play-by-play you read in *What Casinos Don't Want You to Know* reflected the way I played in those earlier years. Let me tell you more about it.

First of all, it is not mathematically smart to convert come bets to place bets or buy bets. The percentage against you on come bets with double odds, as we learned in the first chapter of this book, is less than on buy bets or place bets. So, that is precisely how I began my play—with a pass line bet with double odds, and an indeterminate number of come bets with double odds, perhaps one, perhaps none. My hope was that the shoot would last long enough for me to gently increase the number of come bets to fill up all the point numbers. Then, a little off-and-on action and I was off to the races.

In those days when I was fully entrenched in a hot hand, I did convert the come bets to place bets and buy bets. With sizeable profits already realized, I was not so concerned about percentages against me as I was about maximizing my payoffs.

At that critical juncture where I believed I might have been in the middle of a good shoot, the conversion to place bets and buy bets had become routine for me. And there were five reasons for doing it:

1. If I was getting a feel good instinctive reaction to the shoot, I wanted to have all the numbers always working to maximize profits.
2. I didn't want to lose on a craps in the come.
3. I didn't want to lose all my come bets (less odds) with a come out 7.
4. The place bets and buy bets paid better. (Even though the percentages are higher on place bets and buy bets, the payoffs are better. A $300 place bet on 6 pays $350 at 7 to 6 odds. But a $100 flat bet with a $200 odds bet pays only $340—even money on the $100 and 6 to 5 on the $200). Not a big deal difference, but a difference, nonetheless.
5. It was simply easier to have place bets and buy bets working than to continuously load up the come.

Incidentally, it is common for most casinos to make odds bets and place bets off (not working) on the come out. The player, however, can make the bets work on the come out by simply telling the dealer, "All my bets work on the come out."

I want to make it clear that I never began a game with buy bets or place bets. I didn't recommend it then, and I certainly don't recommend it now. But I saw nothing wrong with making the conversion after I was witness to the making of a good shoot.

Today, however, I trust in my Power Betting Strategy and follow it faithfully, which means no place bets, no buy bets. Frankly, I enjoy riding the progression on as few as two or three come bets much more than loading up the point numbers with

place bets. And for me, the change has paid off. You can't argue with percentages.

Incidentally, there's another Michigan gambler out there who played a pivotal role in my change of habit years ago. He was next to me at a dice table in Atlantic City, telling me about his favorite gambling book, Casino Games.

"That's a good one," I said, "and if you have it with you, I'll autograph it for you."

"Yeah, you do look like the author," he said, "I remember that picture of you in a green jacket, right?"

"Right. My Masters jacket."

"You know, you're not playing like you say in your book. You've got place bets out there on the 5 and 9, yet you only recommend the pass line and come bets."

And he was right. Even though I preached pass line and come bets, pass line and come bets, I had developed the habit of eventually converting the comes.

"Well, my come bets hit twice on both numbers. So, now I want to keep the bets up with place bets. I feel I'm over the hump with this shooter, and I want to be in position to win on that number if it rolls again. Streaks, you know."

"Yeah, but… I follow your advice religiously, and here you are making place bets."

"Hey, go ahead and follow my book," I said. "That's fine. In fact, you're playing smarter than I am."

He walked away feeling a little disillusioned in meeting me. I could tell. I walked away disillusioned, too. But a little smarter.

QUESTION: What should I do with my come bet if I had built it up to, say, $100, and then it won again for the last time with a seven-out. Shouldn't I take it down to pre-play since there will be a new shooter coming out, and the table has been cleared of all other bets? That seven-out, even though it won my come bet, ends the progression, right?

ANSWER: No. Don't take the come bet down to pre-play. It didn't lose! That's called, "Shooting the winning horse." It should proceed up the progression with your next opportunity to make a come bet after the next shooter has established a point number to shoot for. This tactic can produce some interesting scenarios. Let me give you my favorite example. This memorable event happened at the MGM Grand in Las Vegas:

Like you, I had a bet sitting in the come when the shooter sevened-out. I lost the pass line bet, and I lost my other come bet that was sitting on the 10. The pass line bet was not very large, so it was relegated back to pre-play. The other come bet was small, too, so I decided to hold off on a second come bet, if I got that far, and just go with two bets to play for the next shooter: the pass line and my lone come bet that was still riding up the ladder.

Here's what happened.

I'm sitting with a meager $5 on the pass line and, of course, $10 in odds. The shooter's point, as I recall, was 6. So out goes my come bet, still in the progression, at $200. It looked a little strange. A lousy nickel on the line, and two blacks in the come. Well, the shooter sevened-out right away so I lost my $15 on the pass line but won the come bet and racked up $400.

Here we go again with another shooter, and I put another $5 on the pass line. He throws a point of 8 so I put up the $10 in odds, and then I shock everyone at the table by neatly placing three black chips in the come. Guess what? The table had obviously turned cold because this shooter, like the other shooter, immediately sevened-out to the groans of everyone at the table. My come bet just turned into a nifty $600!

A third shooter, and the same story. He made a point, then sevened-out. And I had $400 in the come! I'm telling you, other players at the table thought I had ESP working for me. They couldn't understand it. With the pass line wagers losing, with no shooter being able to string together any point numbers, everyone thought the table was cold. It was, but not for everyone. To the come bettor, it was a short, but hot shoot!

It was not just a matter of timing. Not at all. It was a matter of following a very good strategy. Power Betting made over $5,000 for me on that memorable day in Vegas, at a table where everyone else was taking a bath!

I'm sure this story will help you remember the answer to the question about whether or not to take down a winning come bet on a seven-out. No! Stay with the progression! I can't promise you'll have the degree of success that I had that day, but you might. And if you do, there's a fringe benefit to go along. The act of winning, when everyone else is losing, is the biggest confidence builder I can imagine.

QUESTION: I had a case making multiple come bets where a bet on the 10 hit and I went back on the come with $50 but lost it there with a craps. So, I reboot the bet in pre-play and go with a nickel on the come. The next number is 4, but I already had a $50 come bet sitting on the 4. So, the dealer puts my nickel on the 4, I give him ten bucks for odds, and now I'm wondering what to do with the payoff on the 4.

ANSWER: Here's the way to think it through: Your 4 hit, so you pocket the profits and go back on the come at the next progression level of $75. Your new bet on the 4 of $5 needs $10 odds and you're all set for the next roll. Even though the bets—one big one and one little one—both took a rest on the 4, they must be thought of as separate bets. Don't let the fact that the bets seemed to trade places confuse you.

QUESTION: If I'm in the progression, should I increase my bet in the come when I have an "off and on"?

ANSWER: No. Don't treat an off-and-on as a progression increase for the bet you had in the come. Technically, the bet sitting in the point box (the bet that won) should be pushed up to the next progression level, but you really shouldn't do that, so you'll just have to let it pass as a repeat option. The only thing you could do that would make any sense is to increase the odds bet, but you only could do that if you're playing at a triple odds (or more) table.

Off-and-on action doesn't happen very often because if you have a come bet out on a number, it's unlikely your next come bet would be exactly the same as your flat wager. Both bets would had to have matched the same level in your progression, and that happens only rarely.

To refresh your memory, a simple "off and on" action happens whenever a point number is rolled for which you have a come bet sitting in a point box and, at the same time, another bet of the same flat amount, sitting in the come. In typical off-and-on action, the dealer merely pays you the winnings on your come bet (placing the chips beside your bet in the come), instead of going through all the unnecessary actions of returning your come bet from the point box to the come, paying it off, and then moving your bet in the come to the same point box and then taking your odds for that bet. The net difference is the winnings on the original come bet, and that's what he pays. Like all come bet payoffs, the dealer makes off-and-on payoffs in the come, too. You should pick up these chips immediately because they are considered a live bet for the next roll.

QUESTION: If I hit a nice come bet that was on the 10, and then I make my next bet on the come to follow the progression, it seems to me that I'm betting too much? With a 2 to 1 payoff on my double odds, that seems like too big an increase to me.

ANSWER: Of course it is! You don't bet the whole shebang, for goodness sakes! Simply bet at the next level in the progression and put all your extra "profit" chips in the tray in front of you. Or put them in your pocket, in your shoes, hide them in your shorts—I don't care what you do with them, but don't bet them right back!

I think I see where you might have been confused. In the text discussion, I said that the progression bets, and the pre-play bets for that matter, are flat wagers that must be backed up with full double odds when the shooter is going after a point number. I don't know how you could have misconstrued that to mean that you bet all of your winnings, including the excess odds payoffs, right back at them.

So, one more time—the wagers on the charts are merely flat wagers. The term flat wager refers to the bet you make on the pass line or in the come on the come-out roll. If the roll is not a point number, the dice are still coming out. The terms double odds and odds bet, refer to the bet you make behind the flat wager on the pass line and the bet you toss to the dealer for him to place on top of your come bet flat wager if and when that bet goes to a point number box.

The dealer, incidentally, will position the odds bet slightly off-center on the stack to distinguish the bet as a come bet and to distinguish the odds bet from the flat wager.

If your bet on the 10, for example, was $25, the next bet you'll make, if that bet wins, will be $50. That's all. That's enough!

QUESTION: When do I go back to the table after I've quit a session? Is waiting ten minutes long enough?

ANSWER: You just don't get it, do you? Under "Explanation of the Rules," I tried to make it clear that the purpose of exiting a session is to stop losses and to retain winnings. If you want to think of the exit as a break, that's fine, as long as you treat it as a legitimate break from the action and can squeeze at least a light lunch into it. Five minutes or 10 minutes or even 15 minutes is not enough, nor is it the real point here. It should take you at least that long to study a table before you actually begin play again. Look at the players; look at the chips in front of them. And do what a friend of mine does: He "pretend plays," as he calls it. He might spend half an hour doing this just to find out he's happy he didn't play.

Promise me you are not going to just walk into the john, do your thing, and walk right back to the same table. That makes a mockery of the Power Betting principles.

Remember to always cash in your chips during your break, and to always start with cash. It provides something substantive to do during the interim. For you, I hope you are always faced with a long line at the counters.

You really are no different from so many other players who simply like to play. I don't share the same enthusiasm you have. I don't have such a great desire to play. I have a great desire to win!

It doesn't take patience to play. But it does take patience to win.

QUESTION: As a conservative bettor, do I restart at the $5 or $10 level when I'm sent back to pre-play?

ANSWER: If you're up $30 or more, you may restart at the $10 level. Rule 3a says you must be able to show a net win of $30 before you can proceed to the $10 wager. Most often, the loss in the progression would not reduce your winnings to less than $30, so restarting in pre-play is usually with a $10 bet.

QUESTION: I've found that I'm never able to enter the progression on a losing wager, which must be a built-in feature of your strategy. So I go mostly by the 3-out-of-3 rule, and I watch for when I'm up $75. Am I right?

ANSWER: Good observation. But there is rhyme and reason to Rule 6, so please do not modify it. Winning three out of four puts you ahead by two unit wagers. The third winning unit in a "win 3/lose 1" series is critical, as any seasoned gambler knows. You will break even if you lose it, or be up the two units if you win it. Like any bet, it's a swing of two units, but in a 4-unit bet it takes on much greater significance. In a race to 4, it's the difference between being tied at 2, or ahead 3 to 1.

The rule does prevent you from entering the progression following a loss. You are absolutely right about that.

I've listed all the combinations for a 4-unit series. In the first combination, you would have entered on the third win (from the 3-out-of-3 rule), so that combination is not relevant here. All combinations not subject to the 3-out-of-3 provision of Rules 4 and 6 for exiting the session or entering the progression are indicated in boldface. It's interesting to note that there are only two such combinations for entering the progression, and only two for exiting the session. Both are listed in Group 4.

4 UNIT SERIES
All Combinations

GROUP 1		GROUP 2	
WWWL	Enter	LLLW	Exit
WWLL	Even	LLWW	Even
WLLL	Exit	LWWW	Enter
LLLL	Exit	WWWW	Enter

GROUP 3		GROUP 4	
WLWL	Even	WLWW	Enter
LWLW	Even	LWLL	Exit
WLLW	Even	WWLW	Enter
LWWL	Even	LLWL	Exit

QUESTION: If odds bets, like you say, only break even over time, what's the point of making them? What difference does it make whether I take single odds or double odds, or any odds at all?

ANSWER: At first blush, your question seems to make sense, but if you think about your options, you'll quickly see that making odds bets is crucial to your chances of success. Your options are to either make bets that will lose over time, or bets that will—or should—tend to even out over time. You really wouldn't want to make just the pass line bets that give the house an advantage, then take a miss on the odds bets that don't give the house an advantage. Would you? Wouldn't you feel a little stupid?

And as far as the difference between single and double odds is concerned, remember from our opening chapter that I like to consider the pass line or come bet combined with the odds bet when determining the house advantage. I like to think of the odds bet as reducing the overall house advantage by dulling the edge of the flat wager on the pass line.

The way you structure your bets, therefore, will make a huge difference over the long term in your bottom line. I would much rather make a $5 bet on the pass line and take $15 in triple odds (if I can get it), than only make a flat wager on the pass line of $20. By taking triple odds on a $5 bet, I've effectively cut the percentage against me by two-thirds! Of course, the casino still holds the full advantage on the come out. But when a point number has been established, I can cut that edge with odds.

Always take the odds!

QUESTION: In *What Casinos Don't Want You to Know*, you recommend "gentle" increases in wagers as a player continues to win. But your Power Betting strategy includes several bets that are full presses of the prior bet level. Please explain.

ANSWER: Gladly. My general recommendation is to always make gentle increases in wagers, beginning perhaps with a 50 to 60 percent increase at the beginning of a nice run, and tapering the increases down a little as the run continues. But that's only a general recommendation. And certainly a conservative one. You would be surprised how many players balk at that recommendation.

Power Betting is a much more aggressive betting strategy than the Gollehon Betting Strategy detailed in *What Casinos Don't Want You to Know* and, accordingly, the strategy is more risky. Power Betting has been revealed in this book as an answer to people who have asked how I specifically bet craps. I follow Power Betting. I accept the risk in exchange for the higher expectations.

Let me repeat what I've said before. If you are the least bit uncomfortable with Power Betting, or with any other aspect of gambling that we've talked about, don't do it. Never do anything that puts you in an uncomfortable position.

Another choice you have is to do additional repeat options such as at the $25 and $50 betting levels. It is in this range of the first level that the risk of the presses is the most significant. As you progress up the ladder, you will obviously reduce your risk as you increase your winnings. Repeat options will help you subsidize that one eventual loss that sends you back down the progression.

QUESTION: What if I lose in the progression on a craps on the come out instead of when a shooter sevens out? Does that count as a loss since I would not have had an odds bet loss, obviously?

ANSWER: Most certainly, it does. I can only hope that when your ultimate loss occurs as you ride the progression, that fateful kiss will happen on the come out, saving you some odds, perhaps megamoney if you were well up the schedule. A loss is a loss. Power Betting does not differentiate among them.

QUESTION: Your progression is interesting. Are you aware that the percentage increases on the conservative side alternate at 50 percent and 33 percent? There's really only one full press, from $25 to $50. That would seem like the only real hurdle to get over. The Aggressive schedule, however, has three full presses, which, I guess, is why it's called "aggressive."

ANSWER: I appreciate your observation. Yes, I'm aware of the symmetry in the progressions. Considerable time and effort went into this strategy.

One of the many advantages of the progression's design is that a player can easily compute the next level beyond those listed. For example, should a conservative player make it to the $600 level, the next level is a 33 percent increase to $800. Next, would be a 50 percent increase to $1200, and so on.

You should also note that the progressions have been designed to make them easier to remember. On the aggressive schedule, it's easy to remember $25, $50, and $75 in the first level; they are just simple increases of $25. The second level of $100, $200, and $300 is the easiest; the incremental increases are $100. The third level is easy, too; each increment is $500.

Here's an extended chart that shows the bets along with their percentages of increase:

POWER BETTING
Progression Increase

CONSERVATIVE		AGGRESSIVE	
$25		$25	
50	100%	50	100%
75	50	75	50
100	33	100	33
150	50	200	100
200	33	300	50
300	50	500	66
400	33	1000	100
600	50	1500	50
800	33	2000	33
1200	50	Table Limit	
1600	33		

6 POWER SHOOTING

It was the summer of 1982, and I was in Reno to research my first book, still in print but now retitled *Commando Craps & Blackjack*. It was there that I met with a host of casino managers and pit bosses to get my facts straight. And it was there that I met my first mechanic. During that year, casinos in Reno and Tahoe had been hit hard by these mechanics—cheaters who had developed a skill in throwing the dice.

I remember when a dice supervisor (that's the politically correct term for pit boss) told me what the shot looks like. "The mechanic slides the dice down the table. They don't turn over. They just slide."

"Yeah, right," I said, "You mean you've got two dealers, a stickman, two boxmen, a pit boss… uh, excuse me, supervisor… all standing around watching this guy slide two dice down the table, and no one thinks something is a little strange?"

"Well, first of all," he says, "the shooter is part of a team; the rest of the team is there to make the bets and distract the personnel."

If there was ever a time for a wisecrack, this was it. "What do these distractors do," I asked, "drop their pants?"

"No, no," he responded, They wait until just before the guy shoots (or should that be slides?) and then they throw out a late bet."

"Well," I replied, "so all the dealer has to do is call out, 'No bet,' and the action's off." But then I realized the error in my reasoning. And the supervisor was quick to point it out.

"Sure, the bet's off, but the roll counts. That's what they want. The big bet was already out. The late bet was just a smoke screen."

So one has to wonder how long the slider keeps throwing. And that was my next question.

"No more than once or twice," he responded. "Hey, we're not stupid, and they're not stupid. A couple of hits and they're out the door—just about the time we're getting a little suspicious. But it's too late."

Someone has to remind the casino bosses of the old adage: Fool me once, shame on you; fool me twice, shame on me.

THE SLIDER'S MOVE

I had to see this to believe it. In those days, the casino's black-and-white surveillance cameras and the low-tech video recorders didn't do much to really bring out the details, but it was there, and it was on tape. Still, I wanted to see it live; I wanted to see a slider in the flesh. A dealer sent me to a friend of his in the racebook, who sent me to another racebook in town where I found the expert shooter.

"You don't work for Gaming Control do ya?" That was the first thing he asked me, a logical response from someone who was just asked if he knows how to slide dice. The Nevada Gaming Control Board employs enforcement officers, or agents, as the casinos call them, to basically keep the games, and the players, honest. The agents wear plain clothes, but not as plain as mine that day. And they also carry a gun. I didn't have a gun. But it was still a good question to ask.

"No. I'm a writer."

"A writer! Hell, am I gonna get paid for this?"

"Uh, no, I just want to learn more about what you do for a book I'm writing."

After feeling each other out, this crusty old gambler softened up a little and told me he'd show me his "trick" shots.

"You want to go to a table?" I asked.

"Here? Hell no! I stay out of casinos."

"Oh."

"I like this place (the racebook) because it has its own entrance. Its got its own parking lot. I don't even see the casino. Here, kid, stick around for this last race, then you can follow me."

"Where we gonna go?" I asked.

"My place."

"Oh."

Thinking that he's going to roll the dice on his living room floor, he interrupts my thinking...

"I've got a table."

So off we go into the foothills of Reno, past the same golf course I had played just days before, winding around to a little subdivision of modest homes. Inside, he guided me to one of his bedrooms, but there was no bed there, just a broken down dice table, the kind that casinos used decades ago, called a "tub" table. It might have been all of eight feet long. When these tables were in use, there was only one dealer, who was also the stickman, positioned at where the boxman is today. Players would gather all around the outside of the table from one end to the other. There was only one section for betting on this old table, unlike the two separate sections at both ends of today's 16- and 18-foot tables. But it worked for him. All he wanted to do was practice.

"Now watch this, kid," said the old man, as the dice scurried down the table.

"Yeah, that's pretty good. But show me how you slide 'em."

"I just did!"

"You did?"

"Yeah, now watch again."

I watched, and I realized what was happening. It was like watching a magician do his trick, over and over, until you finally figure it out. Both dice were indeed sliding down the floor of the table, but they were also spinning. Both dice were spinning so fast that you couldn't see the numbers on top, so you just assumed the roll was legal. The dice spun so wildly and the slide was so fast that if you weren't paying close attention, it looked perfectly normal. Except that the dice didn't bounce off the wall.

So I told him, "Hey, I thought the dice have to bounce off the wall."

"They do. But remember, no one at the table is paying attention to the slide. Oh, maybe just a brief glance. That's the scam. That's how it works. If we think they're getting wise, we scoop up our winnings and blow."

"Oh, yeah, I remember. Another player or two gets the dealer's attention just before you throw, right."

"Absolutely. And there are always two. One for each end of the table."

"So," I asked, "do you do this anymore?"

"Naw, I'm getting on in my years. Hell, I'm 75! Besides, I'm working on another shot."

"Oh yeah? Let me see it."

"What number do you want, kid?"

"Uh, 11."

"One 11 coming right up."

This time, the guy spins the dice in the air, not sliding them across the table, and they land on 9, fifty-four. He got the 5, but he missed the 6.

"Let me try it again."

The dice spun out of his hand so fast you could hear them sing, and one die literally stuck on the table with a 5 up, but the other die tumbled to a 3.

"Like I said, I'm still working on this one. Just watch."

After about five tosses, he made his 11, then he made it again.

"I like this a lot better because I don't need a team of idiots to help me. I can go it alone."

Sensing a little friction with his team members, thinking there might have been some problems splitting up the booty or something, I asked him why it was so important to try a shot you could make without needing anyone else to help.

"Somebody screws up and we're cooked." Then he looked at me with an expression that said, "Talk about something else."

So I did. And I went back to the "hitting the wall" problem. "With this spin-shot, the dice still don't hit the wall, and it's too slow to be able to distract the dealers. Besides, you couldn't possibly perfect this shot to the point where you can name your number and hit it every time."

"Right on all counts. I can get away with not hitting the wall a couple of times. Maybe three or four times. But I'm not going to milk it. I don't want to lose my shooting privileges. Besides, the shot looks legit, so I don't need to distract anyone. And as far as your other question is concerned, I'm not going to go for an 11. That's a one-roll bet. I'll make a big bet on a hard 6 or 8 where I have at least a few chances to hit it. I'm looking for a high-odds payoff, but I need four or five shots at it."

"You've got it all figured out, don't you? I'm impressed. But how could you still have any shooting privileges left up here?"

"Oh, I might have to go to Vegas again. But maybe not. My son's pretty good at it, too."

"You're teaching your son your new shot?"

"Yeah, and he's teaching me one. Watch this."

So this gruff old character goes back to the slide-shot, but this time one die is spinning on the floor of the table as it slides, and the other die is tumbling on top of it. One die is controlled, the other is not. The shot was very effective.

"That's got to be more difficult to detect," I commented. "But isn't it much less of an advantage knowing that you've got a 1 in 6 chance of losing?"

"Not really," he said. "Let's say we kill the 5 (put the 5-spot up) and wheel the 5 with the 1, the 3, the 4, and the 5. Now, we've got bets out on the 6, 8, 9, and 10. Out of six ways, we've got one way to lose (5-2), one way that's nothing (5-6), and four ways to win (5-1, 5-3, 5-4, and 5-5). Damn good odds, I'd say! And I'm tempted to try it on my own."

He could probably have gotten away with it. Especially at some tables I've played where the dealers acted like zombies, not even looking at the dice, just waiting for the stickman's call to either pay bets or take them away. They couldn't have cared less about a slider; all they cared about was when their shift ended.

And the bosses aren't the problem, either. I've seen bosses harassing cocktail waitresses, writing markers, and whispering sweet nothings in the ear of the pit girl who runs the computer for them. And in many instances, I've seen them just basically standing around, staring out into space, with their thoughts a hundred miles away.

Bosses aren't the guys they worry about. And it's not the dealers. It's the boxmen. Some tables have two boxmen, some only have one. Obviously, with this guy's new slide, he would want to look for a table with only one boxman. And I'm sure he could come up with some way to distract the boxmen and the stickman at the same time. Otherwise, he might have had to break down and put his team back together, even with his beautiful "one die spins, one die tumbles on top" routine. It's hard to get impressed with the skill of a cheater. It's hard for me to really appreciate any kind of scam. But I've got to tell you, this guy's shot was a thing of beauty.

No question about it. This new shot was a stunning improvement over the common slider. An improvement, indeed.

But there's more to these guys than just perfecting their shot. What's just as interesting about them is the way they operate, the way they set up their victims.

THE SLIDER'S TECHNIQUE

The quickness of the action is equally impressive. The slider positions the dice in either the field or the come and fumbles with them as any rank amateur might do. He's leaning over the table considerably to do this, and that unusual posture is something that dealers should be on the lookout for. He leans over because he wants to slide the dice down the center of the table, which, in itself, is also unusual and should be another warning sign. The success of the trick rides on the slider's trigger finger. Just as you expect him to continue playing with the dice, the trigger is pulled and the shot is finished before you even realize what happened.

As a team, the slider and his cronies are choosy about the table and the casino. They already know from past experiences who's sharp and who isn't. And they look for a dead table. They don't want a bunch of chips scattered all over that might interfere with the slide.

Usually, the slider will position himself directly to the stickman's left (if the slider is right-handed). A team member will go to the extreme left end of the table in order to take the dealer at 2nd base out of the shot. He also is supposed to "turn" the boxman watching that end of the table. Just before the slide, he'll throw some money down or yell out a call bet to turn the heads of the dealer and the boxman at the shooter's end of the table. Of course, the big bets have already been made on the wheeled numbers. The other team member positions himself directly across the table from 3rd base, which puts him on the other side of the stickman. Since he's at the end of the table where the dice are heading, his job is critical. He must distract the dealer, the other boxman, and the stickman by making a late bet or screaming something that can't help but get their attention for that instant of time until the dice are sitting by the wall, waiting for a nice payoff.

Today, casino surveillance people call these mechanics by different names, depending on the type of shot they use. If both dice slide, whether they're spinning or not, the shot is called a **slide**, and the shooter is called a **slider**. Basically, a slider controls both dice.

If, however, only one die slides, whether it's spinning or not, and the other die tumbles, the shot is called a **scoot** and the shooter is called a **scooter**. Even though only one die is controlled, the scoot team is number one on the casino's surveillance list. Since the shot is hard to detect, a casino could lose thousands to a scoot team in just a matter of minutes.

And finally, there is the **spinner** and his remarkable spin-shot in the air. The spinner tries to control both dice, but as we've learned, it's a skill shot that doesn't work every time. A surveillance director I talked to called this shot "The Helicopter," and said he doesn't see it very often anymore. When it works, both dice will "stick" to the floor when they hit, based on the gyroscopic principle that keeps airplanes level. The dice spin so fast that they stay on the same plane of rotation, all but ensuring, in theory, a perfect kill shot.

I don't know where the old man from Reno is today, or even if he's still alive. But I'm sure he's had a few "no rolls" called on him since then, by a sharp boxman or stickman, or maybe even an alert pit boss who was too young to know that it's okay to bother the cocktail waitresses. "No roll." That's the first and most effective countermeasure the casino can use against these cheaters while they're in action. But once they get the scam on tape, look out.

THE SHARPSHOOTER'S MOVE

In the summer of 1985, I ventured back to Reno for research. There was a particular attraction to Northern Nevada for me, besides the obvious beauty of the High Sierras. I spent considerable time in Vegas doing research, too, but the Reno/Tahoe area seemed to bring out the real experts at the games, and casino managers and bosses who would talk more freely. I had always found that more information could be gleaned from Northern Nevada than from its upstaging sister down south. Sports betting was a good example. Even to this day, I'm convinced that the best sports handicappers are concentrated in Northern Nevada. At that time, there was no question that the best dice mechanics were there, too.

It was three years since my last visit, and dice "experts" had thinned out a bit. But I wasn't there for that reason; in fact, I had made the tough decision to simply file away all I had accumulated on these guys, using only a wisp of the data for *Commando Craps & Blackjack*. My reason was valid: *Commando* was carefully crafted for both beginners and experienced players. But a section or two on dice scooters would fall under the heading of advanced text. It just didn't seem to fit.

And wouldn't you know it? While picking up some tips on baseball betting, I stumbled onto a story about a dice player who was teaching his buddies how to spin the dice a different way. The scuttlebutt around town was that the technique didn't look so obvious and didn't stir up the wrath of surveillance

people. I had to check him out, especially since he would be so easy to find. He worked at a casino!

When I found him, it was immediately clear that his technique wasn't the only thing that was different. He was different, too. For one, he was a young kid and talked a mile a minute. He wanted to talk about his newfound success, unlike my first encounter with a dice mechanic. I couldn't shut him up. In fact, he wanted to show me the whole act—not at his home, not at a coffee shop, but at the dice tables! He came off as a screwy, mixed-up kid, but I wanted to see what he could do. Besides, he said he knew "a little something" about baseball.

He picked the sleaziest joint in Reno to show me his stuff. He got the dice and put $20 (money plays) on the pass line. He hit a 7 and now had some chips to play with. Another $20 and another 7. He was up a quick $40. His point became 8 and he made it in three tosses. Six the point. Six right back. This guy was starting a roll. And let me tell you, he acted nothing like the mouthy kid I had just met earlier. He was all business. And when I asked him something at the table, he always gave me the same curt response: "Not now." He was an actor, and he was in his role.

All I could learn from his shooting was the way he set the dice. I knew he was setting them, but he was as smooth as a card shark. And the spin was indeed different. He wasn't going for a stick shot, where the dice stick on certain numbers. In fact, he wasn't spinning them horizontally to make that work; he was spinning the dice vertically. The dice spun side by side, not one above the other. And when they would come down from a rather high arc, each die would hit the layout just inches apart, then lunge forward like top spin on a cue ball. Few of his shots hit the wall, but they usually ended up right at the interface of the table floor and the wall. For the dealers at this particular casino, it was close enough.

Surprisingly, he didn't have a spectacular shoot, so it was a good thing I didn't jump in late. I just wanted to watch; I had not planned on playing. He made about five passes, with an unusually high number of 6s and 8s. He sevened out going after a 4. But he made money, about three hundred dollars. And as we walked away from the table, he started talking again.

It didn't take long for me to realize what he was doing. He was playing a variation on the old blanket roll, a common scam in private games and in the Service. As we talked, it became increasingly obvious that he didn't really know the mathematics behind his technique. He knew what to do, but he didn't really know why. It was obvious someone else had taught him his trick. But one thing was certain: He was good at it! I asked him where he picked up on it, but I never got an answer. I asked him how long it took him to master it, and I got the answer I expected: "I practice a lot." I concluded that this guy must have practiced a long time.

In Reno, you can still find a lot of 25-cent games. So, unless he had a table at home like the first guy, practicing in the real world did not have to be expensive.

When we parted company, I remember telling him he was one of the best dice mechanics I had ever seen. He frowned a little and told me not to call him a mechanic. "I hate that word," he said. Call me "The Sharpshooter."

He didn't like my laugh, but he liked my comeback: "Kind of like 'Billy The Kid,' huh?"

ANALYSIS OF THE SPIN-SHOT

Here's the way his spin-shot works, and why it works. Pick up a die and hold it so that your right thumb is on the 6-spot, and your third finger is on the 1-spot. Position the die so that the 2-spot is facing straight up. Now, visualize an axis passing through your fingers on which the die will spin. Using the forefinger on your left hand, gently spin the die to simulate the die rolling down the table. As the die turns, note the four faces that appear: the 2, 3, 5, and 4, in that order. If you were to carefully roll this die on a soft blanket on the floor, it is possible to keep the die rolling along this 6-1 axis so that when the die stops rolling, either the 2, 3, 5, or 4 will be up. In other words, the 6 and the 1 have been taken out of play.

Note the following chart that shows the three different axes of rotation.

AXIS OF ROTATION		
AXIS		
5-2	**3-4**	**6-1**
1	1	2
3	2	3
6	6	5
4	5	4

(Row labels: **FOUR ROTATIONAL FACES IN PLAY**)

In reality, it is too difficult to roll just one die in such a controlled manner, but it is relatively easy to do this with two dice that are held tightly together, as if two faces were glued squarely together. The forefinger, third finger, and ring finger are used to spin the die from their sharp edges; the little finger and thumb are used to hold the dice tightly and squarely together.

And, with two dice, there are obviously two sets of two numbers that are taken out of play. By preventing two numbers on each die from coming up, the shooter has drastically changed the randomness of the game. Each set of numbers always total 7, since they represent opposite sides of a die (opposite sides always total 7: 6-1, 5-2, and 3-4).

Here's another chart that shows the total of all combinations that can occur by rolling the dice on selected axes, thereby keeping the axis numbers out of play.

DICE COMBINATIONS							
ROLL	**SUM**	**ROLL**	**SUM**	**ROLL**	**SUM**	**ROLL**	**SUM**
5-2, 5-2 SET							
1-1	2	3-1	4	6-1	7	4-1	5
1-3	4	3-3	6	6-3	9	4-3	7
1-6	7	3-6	9	6-6	12	4-6	10
1-4	5	3-4	7	6-4	10	4-4	8
3-4, 3-4 SET							
1-1	2	2-1	3	6-1	7	5-1	6
1-2	3	2-2	4	6-2	8	5-2	7
1-6	7	2-6	8	6-6	12	5-6	11
1-5	6	2-5	7	6-5	11	5-5	10
6-1, 6-1 SET							
2-2	4	3-2	5	5-2	7	4-2	6
2-3	5	3-3	6	5-3	8	4-3	7
2-5	7	3-5	8	5-5	10	4-5	9
2-4	6	3-4	7	5-4	9	4-4	8
5-2, 3-4 SET							
1-1	2	3-1	4	6-1	7	4-1	5
1-2	3	3-2	5	6-2	8	4-2	6
1-6	7	3-6	9	6-6	12	4-6	10
1-5	6	3-5	8	6-5	11	4-5	9
3-4, 6-1 SET							
1-2	3	2-2	4	6-2	8	5-2	7
1-3	4	2-3	5	6-3	9	5-3	8
1-5	6	2-5	7	6-5	11	5-5	10
1-4	5	2-4	6	6-4	10	5-4	9
6-1, 5-2 SET							
1-2	3	3-2	5	6-2	8	4-2	6
1-3	4	3-3	6	6-3	9	4-3	7
1-5	6	3-5	8	6-5	11	4-5	9
1-4	5	3-4	7	6-4	10	4-4	8

If we total up all the combinations and compare them to a random toss, the results are astounding. Instead of 36 combinations in a random game, there are now only 16 combinations regardless of which pair of axis numbers is taken out of play. But more important than the diminished number of combinations is the distribution of these combinations to make certain point numbers, as we'll soon see. The following chart lists all the combinations that are possible:

FREQUENCY OF NUMBERS (PROBABILITIES)											
NUMBER	2	3	4	5	6	7	8	9	10	11	12
RANDOM	1	2	3	4	5	6	5	4	3	2	1
5-2, 5-2 SET	1	0	2	2	1	4	1	2	2	0	1
3-4, 3-4 SET	1	2	1	0	2	4	2	0	1	2	1
6-1, 6-1 SET	0	0	1	2	3	4	3	2	1	0	0
5-2, 3-4 SET	1	1	1	2	2	2	2	2	1	1	1
3-4, 6-1 SET	0	1	2	2	2	2	2	2	2	1	0
6-1, 5-2 SET	0	1	1	2	3	2	3	2	1	1	0

Notice in particular the 6-1, 6-1 set. There are no combinations that will yield a craps! With both 6s and both 1s out of play, there is no way to roll 1-1, 1-2, 2-1, or 6-6. This is clearly the right set for the come-out roll. And, once a point is established, it can be determined from this chart which set is the best to use.

If the point number is either 6 or 8, the 6-1, 5-2 set is the right choice. In fact, if you convert the combinations to odds, you'll be shocked to find out that the normal 6 to 5 negative odds have been skewed to plus odds of 2 to 3! Instead of six times you lose to five times you win, the odds have been flipped over to two times you lose and three times you win! If you're not clear how we got it, look at the distribution of combinations on the 6-1, 5-2 set. Under either the 6 or 8, there are three combinations. Under the 7, there are two combinations. Since odds are always expressed with the first number representing an event (a pass) not happening (a 7 resulting in a loss) we have correctly found odds of 2 to 3. Such odds translate into a 60 percent win frequency. Not too shabby.

A further advantage of the 6-1, 6-1 come out set is the greater likelihood of a point number being either a 6 or 8, which, as we just saw, are the point numbers with the 60 percent likelihood of making. Such a sweet deal. If the point number is 4 or 10, the 3-4, 6-1 set works the best because there are two ways to make either the 4 or 10 compared to two ways to make the 7. Instead of bucking odds of 2 to 1, the shooter has an even money chance of winning.

If the point number is 5 or 9, any set that is not identical works. But, of the non-identical sets, the 5-2, 6-1 set is probably used so that the shooter can also place the 6 or 8 and get that nice 60 percent win rate working for him.

Here are the charts that sum it all up for us.

PROPER SETS	
COME OUT	6-1, 6-1
POINT 6 OR 8	6-1, 5-2 (AND FOR 6 OR 8 PLACE BETS)
POINT 4 OR 10	3-4, 6-1
POINT 5 OR 9	6-1, 5-2 (AND FOR 6 OR 8 PLACE BETS)

Now you can see why using a blanket was one of the most effective scams in a private dice game. Of course, casino bosses know all about this, too, so don't think for a moment that some pit boss will let you spread out a blanket on the table the next time you want to shoot craps. But "The Sharpshooter," or rather, the guy who taught him, figured out a way, without using a blanket, to work the same scam on a full-size, regulation, casino dice table.

The theory is based on the same gyroscopic principle that we talked about originally in the case of the "helicopter" spin-shot, except that the dice are not stacked vertically but held horizontally. And the object is not to make the dice stick to the floor on a certain number, but to keep the dice perfectly balanced along the same axis of rotation from the minute they leave the mechanic's hand, through the bounce on the table, and throughout the top-spin roll to the wall.

To be successful at this, the dice must spin so rapidly that they are merely a blur as they shoot through the air. Keeping them spinning is what prevents them from tilting out of kilter. Of course, the dice must leave the mechanic's hand perfectly level, and that's the real trick. What does it take? I think it takes the same thing my old piano teacher used to preach: practice, practice, practice.

When I watched "The Sharpshooter," I couldn't tell exactly how he was holding and spinning the dice, but it was certainly different from the old blanket roll. I have no idea how he produced such a fast-spinning action. I'm certain, however, that I figured out the idea behind this guy's special shot. The charts should prove my theory. Hopefully, this study will help casino managers educate their dice crews so they can spot such a shooter before he can do any damage.

Don't get me wrong. I don't mind seeing someone beat the casino, but I want to see him doing it the way we all do it. Against the odds.

What's interesting about this story, for me, at least, is the mathematical theory of the shot. And let's be serious for a moment. The charts show how the common blanket roll works on paper. That's all it shows. I'm not entirely convinced that it can work in the casino. Maybe "The Sharpshooter" was just lucky for ten minutes.

Maybe not.

EPILOGUE

My investigation into the world of power shooters has certainly been no secret. While on a recent gambling trip, I got an urgent call in my room from a boss downstairs in the dice pits. "John, come on down here! I want you to see this guy! Tell me what he's doing!"

He sounded excited—and worried. So I hurried down and joined him in the pit. I was wearing a nice suit that day—business meetings, you know—so here I am standing in the pit with two other bosses watching a dice game, and I would have to believe I looked like a boss, too. That's probably the closest I'll ever come to being a bona fide pit boss.

Anyhow, we watched this kid for a few minutes and he was throwing a lot of numbers—and he was spinning the dice. He'd hit the wall enough times that there wasn't much the bosses could do about him. And he was costing the casino thousands. From what I could gather, it was their first experience with a spinner, and they didn't know how to handle it.

SUMMATION

ODDS	WIN C/O	LOSE C/O	EST PT C/O	REPEAT 6-8	REPEAT 4-10, 5-9
CONTROLLED	3-1 (25%)	0 (0%)	1-3 (75%)	2-3 (60%)	1-1 (50%)
UNCONTROLLED	7-2 (22%)	8-1 (11%)	1-2 (66%)	6-5 (45%)	2-1 (33%)

EST PT C/O: ESTABLISH POINT ON THE COME-OUT

This chart compares controlled (blanket roll) to uncontrolled percentages. For example, the likelihood of winning on the come-out (C/O) with controlled dice is 25 percent, compared to 22 percent for uncontrolled. The 7 to 2 odds for uncontrolled is simply the total of all ways of winning, 8 (six ways for a 7, and two ways for an 11), versus the remaining 28 combinations that don't immediately win (36 minus 8).

If you learn anything from all this, you've just learned that you have only a 22 percent chance of winning outright on the come-out roll in a random game. Even with controlled dice, the odds of an outright win are not that much better. The big benefits to the blanket-roll scam are the 0 percent chance of an outright loss, the 50 percent chance of making points of 4, 5, 9, or 10, and particularly the 60 percent chance of making points 6 or 8.

I took a different tack. "Check his ID," I told them.

"What? What do you mean?"

"He looks 19. Go check him."

Rusty, the floorman who got the assignment, walked over to him, told the stickman to stop the game for a moment, and asked the kid to show his driver's license.

He went through a bunch of cards before he got to his driver's license.

How old was he?

He was 19.

The dice passed to the next shooter, and the kid was out the door.

A few handshakes, a pat on the shoulder, and I was out of the pit, mumbling all the way to my room, "He'll be back. He's too good to stay away."

In all but half a dozen notable exceptions, I was not that impressed with the knowledge of the surveillance people I had met, and I was convinced they were not stonewalling me. It could also have been that they wanted to suppress any publicity about these guys. I think they knew that spinners could be a real problem. Not the scooters and sliders who were blatantly cheating. No, they weren't the problem. The spinners, on the other hand, had perfected a skill, a real skill, but the statutes still considered spinning as a cheat move. Again, the parallel to the days of blackjack card counters was striking.

Shortly after my book was released, I was contacted by FOX News in a follow-up to newspaper stories in the *Las Vegas Sun* and the *Review Journal*. The matter wasn't suppressed anymore. Now, anyone would know that spinners exist, and they exist in force.

The first question I was always asked in an interview was, "Are you a dice mechanic?" And I would tell them, "No. Absolutely not. I'm a writer. I simply have an interest in the topic."

One of the newspaper reporters misquoted me in his story and said that I had used trick shots at a big Strip hotel. The only time I actually spun the dice at a casino, the incident the reporter was talking about, was in the early morning at a Strip hotel with a crew who knew me and knew that I was investigating mechanics. They wanted to know how I was doing, and I told them. Since there wasn't a game going at that particular table, I told them to give me the dice, call out a number, and I'd show them a spin-shot. I thought I'd need a few tries at it, but, as luck would have it, the dice stuck on the number on the first toss. The crew was stunned.

The pit bosses had been watching. They told the crew, "Watch him closely when he's shooting for real!" I'm sure they knew my interests in cheat shots were purely journalistic. I never had any interest in actually using my "skill" to win money. But that warning to the crew still nags at me, just as I'm sure it nagged at blackjack card counters over two decades ago.

The only other time I was involved, sort of, in a dice-spin incident turned out to be more of a joke than a serious encounter. During a photo shoot for my book at another hotel, on a closed dice table, a player who knew the scoop kept pestering me about the spin-shot. He finally got what was coming to him. I showed him the "Helicopter." He played around with it on the table while the photographer was setting up his camera. He threw the dice a few times and made a jerk of himself. He told me he had mastered the shot—in five minutes?—and scurried off to the nearest open table.

When I finished up with the photographer, I spent a few minutes with the hotel's publicity director, then decided to walk around the tables to see if I wanted to play before dinner.

At the busiest table of all is this same jerk, at the center of attention, about to throw his very first spinner in a real, live dice game. I watched him screwing around with the dice, sweating and fidgeting with the cubes, totally unsure of himself. "Throw 'em," yelled other players. "Pick 'em up and shoot 'em," said the floorperson. And off they went, flying high and hard, from one end of the table to the other, right into the dealer's face. One of the dice actually cut the dealer's nose.

You see, to get the spin, the dice are stacked vertically, resting on the little finger, while held by the corners with three curled fingers. A simple whip action with the wrist sends the dice flying out of your hand with a sizzling spin. But to a right-handed novice, they tend to fly off to the right. Just like my golf ball.

Well, so much for playing before dinner. I couldn't stop laughing.

7 CASINO COUNTERMEASURES

So what does a casino manager do when he finds a dice mechanic plying his trade on the casino's dice tables? It's actually a pretty good question. The answers I got from several casino managers and surveillance directors varied all over the place. Clearly, each casino has its own policies. Here's an assortment of answers:

"We take his shooting privileges away."

"Take his picture."

"We kick him out."

"Try to put him in jail."

"We show him the door."

"Prosecute."

Funny how every answer I got used the masculine pronouns, "him" or "his." And it was no accident. Of all the mechanics who have ever been suspected, not a single one was a female. Such a nice tribute to the women's movement. But one particular comment stuck in my mind: "We've never tried to have them arrested at any of our properties. What we do is stop 'em. Our dealers know exactly what to do."

Maybe so, but I certainly have my doubts. It's true that a good stickman, sensing a slide-shot coming up, can stop the roll by hitting the dice with his stick. That action constitutes "no roll" just as if any member of the crew would have called

"no roll." It's also true that once a mechanic knows the dealers are on to him, he has no chance of succeeding.

Another interesting comment I got came from Dick Favero, casino manager at the popular Palace Station in Las Vegas. Favero told me that they must call "Gaming" whenever an incident of suspected cheating takes place. He said gaming statutes require all casinos to make these reports. Apparently, if a casino doesn't report it, it could be cited or fined.

In spite of the lacking of a uniform policy, it's my gut feeling that most of the major casinos are taking a more serious approach. Ron Asher, Chief of Enforcement for the Nevada Gaming Control Board, steered me to a recent case in Northern Nevada where a dice mechanic was actually convicted. "We got the conviction," he said, with a satisfaction in his voice like the golfer who just broke par.

The incident happened at Fitzgeralds in Reno, according to surveillance director, Larry Dennison. But Dennison didn't immediately recall any other convictions against a mechanic, nor did Asher. No one else I spoke with could recall one, either. But my suggestion to anyone who's thinking about playing against these guys is "Look out!" They'll make you shoot from the championship tees!

One interesting fact I learned from Dennison is the high level of communication shared among surveillance people. Dennison is president of the Northern Nevada Surveillance Network, which networks with other surveillance groups not only in their own state but throughout the country. And that would seem especially important now with the explosion of gaming in every nook and cranny of the United States.

It's important to realize that dice mechanics are considered out-and-out cheaters, no different from a cheater trying to rig a slot machine. A mechanic is no less a cheater than some guy who walks in with his own phony dice.

CASINO COUNTERMEASURES

I had a brief encounter with a dice mechanic in 1989 in Las Vegas who said he "locks up $300, sometimes $500 a day. And get this: He said he's a totally ethical player. "I don't use balonies (phony dice), no past--posting, nothing like that. I go for the skill element alone. This guy thinks it's okay to slide the dice! He told me he's lived in Vegas for 27 years, and only plays where the bosses let him shoot. And he had to tell me he thinks he's the best around. Here's a self-confessed dice mechanic who compares himself to Joe Montana. Making a comparison between the dubious skill of throwing dice to the real skill of throwing 50-yard touchdown passes is like comparing a rowboat to the Queen Mary!

If this stupid dice mechanic didn't even know he was cheating, you have to wonder how many other honest players think the same.

I found out. It was truly amazing how many of my friends who play didn't know that skill shots at the dice table were illegal. But it's easy to see how this might have gotten misconstrued.

Years ago, skilled blackjack players had to fight for their right to count cards, in an effort to overcome the house edge. Casino bosses in those times, and even some today, looked at a card counter as a cheater. But a card counter wasn't really cheating. He was simply applying a skill to beat the game. And unlike the dice mechanic, the card counter's skill was passive to the actual operation of the game.

So, in the case of blackjack counters, the skill is legal; in the case of dice mechanics, it isn't. And to make it all the more confusing, it's okay now to count cards in your head, but it's cheating to use a device. What's considered cheating in one state might not be in another. It's no wonder that gamblers are such a confused bunch.

Indeed. Some new gaming jurisdictions have not fully defined their statutes. Most of these new jurisdictions would be

wise to follow Nevada statutes. They have been tried, revised, and tested for decades. Here's how the Nevada Gaming Control Board defines "cheat" in statute 465.015:

1. "Cheat" means to alter the selection of criteria which determine:
   a. The result of a game; or
   b. The amount or frequency of payment in a game.

Clearly, if a dice mechanic is able to roll a predetermined number, or at least has a better than random chance of rolling a particular number, he has effectively "altered the selection of criteria." Clearly, the game is no longer random. Clearly, if the game is being watched and taped, this guy is in a peck of trouble.

But the actual process of discovering a mechanic and the decision on what to do can be a little more involved.

Richard (Jerry) Clark, Surveillance Director for Caesars Palace, tells me that the first wave of countermeasures should indeed come from the trenches. That is, the dealers and floor people should be able to spot a mechanic and quickly react. They can temporarily foul up the mechanic's game plan by calling "no roll" if they think the dice are sliding instead of turning over. And they can certainly call "no roll" if they think both dice are not going to hit the wall. But they have to make that call before the dice come to rest.

There's even more they can do. A dealer or pit boss who is suspicious of a shooter, according to Clark, should tell the shooter, "Take your business across the street. We don't want you in here." If the mechanic is playing at Caesars Palace and takes the dealer literally, he'll be heading over to the Flamingo Hilton (right across the street from Caesars) where I'm sure they don't want his business either!

The key things a dice dealer or pit boss can accomplish are making it clear to the mechanic in no uncertain terms that the casino bosses are wise to him. He's been discovered, or at least suspected. And also, quickly and firmly disposing of him. Now that doesn't mean dumping his body in the trash bin. Caesars might be tough on cheaters, but not that tough! The suspected mechanic will be asked to leave and, hopefully, never seen again.

But how does a dice dealer, or a pit boss, or even the surveillance director know for sure that a bona fide, genuine article mechanic is at work? What about the guy who just likes to play with the dice, setting them with a certain number up, or certain numbers on the side? Is this guy a mechanic? We've all done it. For many, it's just a superstition. But where do you draw the line? Later in this chapter, I will tell you a story about a shooter who went through a regular ritual with the dice before he would throw them. In that story, you'll see that the pit boss drew the line a little too closely.

What about the rookie dice player who begins wondering whether or not he can throw a certain number, so he plays around with the idea, having absolutely no inkling that what he's doing is illegal. Is this guy going to get cuffed? And what about the shooter who just doesn't hit the wall every time? We've all done that, too. We roll them two feet short and the dealers look at us like we're a lowlife crook. Said a dealer to a guy who came up short one time too many: "All the way to the end, buddy. This is a game of luck, not a game of skill."

"Oh, excuse me, sir. I'm sorry, sir... (under his breath)... you stupid sonofabitch."

It's not hard to see the difficulty pinpointing the real crooks, and it's not hard to understand why casinos are paranoid about being absolutely certain when they decide to go for the arrest.

That's the top level of action that might be taken. If the pit boss, who first noticed the suspicious roll, calls surveillance

to make sure the tape is running; and if the shooter, thinking he's getting away with it, continues his scam for another few minutes or so; and if the scam is a documented technique such as a scoot-shot, there's a pretty good chance a security guard will detain the suspect while Gaming is called. The casino will have some pretty good evidence on tape.

If the casino thinks it has a good case, it might decide to prosecute. The downside of all this is the difficulty in getting a conviction. If the alleged mechanic demands a jury trial, finds a hot-shot lawyer, and gets an acquittal, you can almost smell a wrongful prosecution lawsuit coming. To arrest, or not to arrest—it's a judgment call depending on how much evidence the casino has to support the charges.

One particular incident that Clark showed me on tape (sent in from another casino) was hard to believe. Here was a scooter, along with his confederates, beating the bejesus out of the casino. He slides the dice, the dealers pay, he slides them again, the dealers pay. It went on and on like this to the point where I commented, "The only way this could happen is if the dealers are in on the scam." And Clark agreed, saying "They're either in on it or they're the dumbest dice crew that's ever been assembled." And the pit boss, we couldn't find him in the tape. He must have been daydreaming about that new cocktail waitress they just hired.

Clark said that in cases like this, where hard evidence of an employee conspiracy doesn't exist but the tape tells the story, sometimes the only thing to do is bargain with the suspects— or let a prosecutor and lawyer do the negotiating—to confiscate the employees' work card. The sheriff's department issues work cards (also called gaming permits) to all employees who work in a casino. Without the card, the person cannot get a job in any casino.

It's a hollow victory for the casino; the suspected employee-thieves bargain away their work card for freedom. No jail, but no more jobs in a casino, either. Of course, if the bad employees are caught red-handed, and the casino can put a good case together, plea-bargaining goes out the window. Not only will the employees lose their workcard, they will very likely lose their freedom.

SPEED BUMPS

In terms of countermeasures to actually prevent a scooter from sliding the dice, George Joseph, the Director of Surveillance for the Bally's properties, has come up with a novel way of thwarting the shot. He designed speed bumps for all of Bally's dice tables that run across the table along both sides of the prop bet layout in front of the stickman. These bumps are about an eighth of an inch high and hardly noticeable. Most important of all, they work like a champ! Scooters now avoid Bally's casinos like the plague.

Why don't all casinos install speed bumps? It's got to be the $64,000 question. Several casino managers I spoke with had never heard of them before. One particular manager told me that it was presented to management and they thought it was too expensive (huh?) and too complicated to install. If you work in a big company, you know what it's like trying to second-guess corporate.

Another response I heard was, "We don't get sliders in here." Maybe they do and they just don't know it. Maybe they rely on their dealers to stop those dice from sliding, but the nice thing about speed bumps is that they're always working.

Kudos to Joseph who also redesigned the paddle (the tool used to push money through the slot in the table and into the drop box) by affixing mirrors to both sides of the handle. When the handle is sitting in the slot, it is positioned perfectly to see opposite sides of a die, just in case a cheater brought his own dice to the game.

SHARP EDGES

Another solid countermeasure, especially for the spin-shots, are the sharp edges produced on casino dice. The manufacturers are instructed by the casinos to make their dice with no measurable radius on the corners. The dice you play Yahtzee with at home are the drugstore variety with rounded corners. They roll nicely on a blanket. Recalling our story about "The Sharpshooter" in the previous chapter, rounded-edge dice would be easier to keep level and on axis when they hit the table and roll.

Sharp corners are more than just a way of ensuring an evenly weighted die. These sharp corners make it difficult to slide dice by catching in the loose top threads of the felt cover. In addition, sharp corners help to randomly deflect the dice as they bounce on the table—a solid countermeasure against spinners.

THE TABLE SURFACE

Still another countermeasure is the design of the dice-table floor. For years, the tables have been designed with only a relatively thin 24-pound felt layout cloth stretched over the table floor. Unlike the blackjack and roulette tables that have a padded layer under the felt, the dice table is a relatively hard surface. The reason for the padded layer on the other tables is so you can pick up chips or cards easier by being able to get your fingernails under them. But on a dice table, that's a bad idea. The harder the playing surface, the more random the bounce.

Until recently, I would have told you that all casinos employ this standard for the floor of their dice tables. But when I played recently at the MGM Grand, I was surprised to find out that their tables had a thick layer of padding under the felt! It made the game considerably quieter (you could not hear the dice bouncing, or even chips hitting the table), but the likelihood of a skilled spinner working those tables is something I'm sure the casino's management will soon remedy.

In the early '80s, many casinos had their dice tables manufactured with a corrugated table floor under the felt. You could feel the convolutions as you brushed your hand over the table. When dice bounce on such a floor, they veer off so randomly, so haphazardly, that a spinner would have no chance of controlling the dice. It totally surprises me that this corrugated floor design is no longer being used.

PYRAMIDS

And we can't forget the wall around the table. Lined with a thick rubber molding designed in a series of pyramids, the wall helps produce a random bounce. But that's assuming the dice hit the wall. Dice mechanics, as we've just learned, ignore the wall. Surprisingly, only a five-inch wide section of the rubber lining incorporates the pyramids, which are one-inch square and one-half inch high. Since the depth of most tables is eleven inches, that leaves six inches of the wall unprotected.

Years ago, I met a physics professor who claimed to be an expert on the randomness of events. His studies, however, dealt more with electrons bouncing around the universe, and gas particles in a test chamber, that sort of fun thing, rather than bones bouncing around on a dice table. I asked him about the spin-shot, both of them, and the effect the rubber pyramids would have in knocking them out of a controlled plane. His

answer might have been a little off the wall, but here's what he said: "If the dice are spinning fast enough, it's possible the pyramids might have only a negligible effect on the rotational axis."

EYE IN THE SKY

Perhaps the most effective countermeasure, especially against the cheater who's a little unsure of himself, is the casino's visible evidence of surveillance. Virtually every player knows about them, because virtually every player has asked about them. I'm talking about those strange-looking black bubbles that hang pretentiously from the ceiling, scattered over the entire casino floor.

Some larger casinos have over 200 of these babies, all being monitored every moment, and all connected to a videotape machine. Casinos like Caesars Palace use a sophisticated multiplex system for taping. In most cases, black-and-white cameras are used because the resolution is sharper. They can zero in on a dime. But color cameras are needed in some cases such as at a roulette table where only a color camera can distinguish the colors of the otherwise identical chips.

The surveillance system is, at the very least, intimidating. And for that reason alone, I'm sure it's worth the huge costs of upkeep. But for the hardened cheaters, nothing intimidates them. It doesn't make any sense, but nothing about them makes any sense. For even the best slider, it might be easy to fake out many a fine dealer, but how do you fake out a camera?

THE DROP SHOT

When surveillance people are watching the games, they're looking for more than just the slider, or the scooter, or the spinner. There are all kinds of scams with dice that drive these people batty. A common trick for a shooter is to kill a number by "accidentally" dropping one of the dice from his hand at the instant he shoots. Actually, the die didn't drop; the shooter carefully placed it on the table in such a way that his hand hid the movement. Invariably, the roll counts. He'll apologize to the dealers for screwing up the shot, and if he looks sincere, they'll believe him.

He can only do that little shot once per table. But there are casinos in Atlantic City that sport 26 dice tables. Foxwoods in Connecticut has 28. Does anyone want to guess how many dice tables are in Las Vegas? Can we stipulate that this "dropper" has a huge market to fleece? It's probably the simplest scam of all, and one of the most difficult to prosecute.

PAST-POSTING

The term **past-posting** comes from the racetrack where years ago it was possible to delay the audio feed of a live horse race to an off-track betting parlor. With an accomplice at the track working the telephone, the past-poster at the betting parlor had the enviable position of knowing the results of a race before the horses went to post. Or so it seemed.

This same scam works in a casino, too. Although it's mostly found at the roulette wheel, the dice table gets its share of past-posters, too. The object of the game is to increase your bet after you already know that the bet won. To do this at a dice table, the player leans out low over the rail, resting one hand on the table, while tossing an eleven or "any craps" bet to the stickman with his other hand. During this subtle distraction, he builds up his pass line bet with a chip or two, or three, hidden in his resting hand.

He must make eye contact with the dealers while he's padding his bet so he can be sure they're not looking at his hand. Some of these guys are so good they can drop as many as three chips on their stack—without looking—while simply moving their hand quickly over the table as if it's a normal action.

Dealers can protect against this scam by keeping an eye on the amount of money each player at their end of the table has wagered. If the dealer knows a player had three black chips on the line with six behind them, and then as he prepares to pay the wager he finds five black chips and ten behind them, he stops, notifies the pit boss, and then gets ready for all hell to break loose.

It's the perfect time to hope that the camera was zeroed in and taping.

RAIL THIEVES

One can only hope that the people watching the monitors in the casino's surveillance room are looking out for the players, too. Obviously, the first and foremost responsibility of the surveillance staff is to protect the casino's assets. However, a good surveillance person will also watch the players at the table, to make sure all payoffs are coming from the dealers, and not from an unsuspecting player standing alongside. Here's how the rail thief works:

When things are busy, and especially when the table's crowded, a good rail thief can reach over to your stash of chips and move a few over to the thief's pocket. Some players are so caught up in the game, especially during a hot shoot, they do nothing to protect the chips in the rail in front of them. Here's what you can do to protect against rail thieves:

Always place your higher denomination chips in the center of your stack. Put a few one-dollar and five-dollar chips on both ends of the stacks. That way, it's more difficult for the thief to fish into the center of your chip stack to find the good ones. If you're playing directly beside the stickman or at the end of the table nearest to the dealers, place the higher denomination chips toward the dealer or stickman. It's a pretty safe bet that the dealers are not going to steal your chips.

If you want to have your chips stolen, just keep playing. Before you know it, all your chips will be gone.

CLAIMERS

Here's another class act for you. How would you like to make your living by claiming someone else's bets at the dice table? I suppose you could say it's a little more "pro" than just reaching over and stealing the chips from a player's rack. It's like a guy at a supermarket checkout lane claiming someone else's food. "Is that my sack of potatoes?" "No. It's mine." "Well, but that's my Jello." "No, that's mine, too." Believe it. There are people sitting around a kitchen table right this moment planning which casino they're going to hit, while eating someone else's Jello.

A pit boss told me years ago that these **claimers** can pull down two to three hundred a night, if they don't get greedy. Greedy? The better crop of claimers actually run it like a business. They're careful not to work the same casino too often, particularly the same shift. In fact, they have a list they follow just to be sure. Of course, it helps if there are a lot of casinos in town, which probably explains why most of these scamsters make Vegas the place they want to raise their kids. Good schools, you know.

The routine works well if the table is busy. It works better if the dealers are inexperienced, or just not paying attention, or both. But it works best if there is another player at the table to back up the claimer. A confederate.

"That's my bet! Not his!" cries the claimer.

"What's he talking about?" says the player who deservingly got his bet paid.

"Sir, you don't have a bet on that number," says the dealer to the claimer."

"The hell I don't! That's my bet! Now pay me!"

And then comes the clincher...

"That's right, sir. It was his bet (the claimer). I saw him make it," fawns the beautiful blonde playing a few spots away. That sensual smile, that affirmative nod—and who can argue?

What the claimer is also relying on, however, is a generous policy of many casinos regarding disputed bets. Casinos don't mind paying winning bets. They're just not crazy about paying them twice. But they do. There are always disputes. The casino's creed is not unlike other "retailers": to keep the customers happy. An admirable policy.

Assuming the bet is not large, say, $25 or so, the casino will generally pay off on a disputed bet, even if it is suspicious, simply to avoid a scene and a resultant stall in the game. Surprisingly, the floorman in charge of the game will not bother the surveillance people, either. Too much hassle to find the right recording device (there are dozens running), stop and recue the action, and play it back—for a measly twenty-five bucks.

Claimers know which casinos are the easiest to take. And they know the limits. Some casinos might give in and pay off a bogus $50 bet, while others might balk at a $6 bet. The claimers know the ground rules from experience. They know how loud they have to argue and how obnoxious they need to get before the floorman says, "Pay him."

A popular scam involves the field bet, and requires a confederate. Stage one is for one of the team members to walk up and plop down a bet in the field, making sure the dealer sees the bet being placed. The field bet is chosen because it's a one-roll wager, meaning there's a win-lose decision on the next roll. The other key necessity of this wager is that it's placed by the player, not the dealer, and can be removed at the player's discretion.

Stage two calls for the second team member to walk up and take a spot beside the other player. To make this scam really look good, the second member appears indecisive by also placing a field bet, picking it up, putting in back on the table, then picking it back up again. At the instant before the dice are launched, this second member picks up the first member's bet. At precisely the same time, the first member distracts the dealer so the pick-up isn't noticed.

Now the casino is stuck. If none of the field numbers hit, the two walk away with the bet. If any field number does hit, the first member complains to the dealer that the other person picked up his bet. Of course, the partner in the scam admits that she (and it usually is a she) accidentally picked up the chips, apologizes, rolls her baby blues, and puts the bet back down on the table. Now the casino is forced to pay off on the bet.

Score one for the team. They're out the door and heading for the next casino on their list.

HEROES OR VILLAINS

Dice is the only game in the casino where the players actually determine the outcome of a betting event. The players produce the numbers. The players expect them to be random. The sliders and scooters we talked about will hurt honest players who are expecting a random game. The players

are getting duped just like the casino. It's an advantage for the players to learn how to spot them.

Frankly, I'm beginning to hate the term "scooter." It's too cute. My neighbor's dog is named Scooter. Let's call these guys what they really are: cheaters. At least that's the way I felt about them until Jack Engelhard came along. Jack wrote *Indecent Proposal*, the much ballyhooed novel that spawned the top-grossing movie in 1993. In his follow-up novel, *Deadly Deception*, which I had the pleasure of publishing, Jack created a most unusual character who had a power to win at the dice tables, a mystical connection to the gods of chance, with a little dice-spinning thrown in for good measure.

But his character is not just your stereotypical power shooter. No sir! Not typical at all because he gives his winnings away! He helps others. And all's fine in 7-11 land until he finds someone not worth helping.

Let's listen in as Jack describes one of the seedier casinos in Vegas where Julian Rothschild, aka, dice mechanic, is about to do his thing:

"Julian's destination was Lucky's, a hole-in-the-wall, sawdust casino, around the corner from Binion's Horseshoe, established during the reign of Bugsy Siegel and still going strong. It was a dump, still with swinging doors and poles outside to tether horses, the last of the honky-tonks, but a marvel to behold for the craps pilgrim making his escape from the new synthetic "family-oriented" complexes along the Strip, top-heavy with kids and slots.

Not a slot in the joint, and what a joint it was. A solitary fan made its reluctant rounds overhead in lieu of air conditioning. There were no signs that said, "Thank You For Not Smoking." The floor stuck to your shoes from bubble gum dropped in the '80s. No Muzak, no band, but somewhere overhead came Frankie Laine and Mule Train. Clippity-clop. Dark, dank, the smell of armpits, cigars, the women straight out of some Lily

Langtry chorus line, the men in pointed boots and ten-gallon hats, the tables brimming with action. This was where craps was meant to be played. Julian had lusted for this. Julian was in his element.

He had come for just that, the action, the purity of it all, which no one but a fellow gambler would understand—would understand that this was where you got lost to find yourself, away from the fraudulence of civilization."

Several casino surveillance people have told me there's a new movie or two coming out that feature dice mechanics. One might even be named Julian Rothschild. Some of the scenes—that the surveillance experts are supposed to review for accuracy—portray the mechanic as a hero, someone to look up to. Apparently, the movie producers have had their fill of blackjack card counters and, like so many other people, think that skilled dice tossing is ethical. If a movie's theme is for some guy to win money by sliding dice, let it be known that he got the money by cheating, not by a rush of luck or respectable skill. He might as well have robbed a bank. But I think Hollywood has done that movie before.

Personally, I have no patience for cheaters—save the Robin Hoods of the casino world like Julian—and I certainly don't want to be standing beside one at a dice table. I enjoy the camaraderie of dice players; we're all bucking tough odds, because we know the playing field is not exactly level. But at least we're playing together.

Dice mechanics, in the real world, anyhow, are only playing for themselves.

WE WANT THE MANAGER!

Earlier in this chapter we talked about average players who like to set the dice on certain numbers, and maybe even try to control the dice by throwing them a certain way. It seems innocent enough, but some pit bosses show little patience. Here's a story that even Ripley can't believe:

It was one of the most bizarre, and memorable, events I've ever witnessed at the dice tables, at one of the Strip's most famous casinos. A high roller had the dice, and he would set them, fumble with them, and play with them, apparently trying to set certain numbers he wanted on top. Then, he would stack them, tap them three times on the table, slide the cubes around in a circular motion, three more taps, and off they went, usually off the table. God, it was a slow game. But there was something very special about this particular shoot. The high roller was having a hell of a hand. Slow, but effective. Everyone was cleaning up; no one minded the slow play. In fact, it was sort of fun to watch the shooter.

But the bosses were watching him, too. And they were mildly irritated at best. After all, the shooter was a prime customer of the hotel. The bosses didn't want to make him angry. If a lowlife had been playing with the dice like that, a boss would have been in his face like a Marine drill-sergeant. Bosses are told to keep the game running. Slowing down the game only slows down the earnings potential of the table. But this table was hot, and it would seem that the bosses should have been happy the table was so slow.

Well, the dice eventually passed to the next shooter, who started setting the dice exactly the same way as the high roller before him. You could see the expression on the boss' face. He was ready to erupt at any moment. But this kid with the copycat routine was getting hotter by the moment. Point after point and the bosses were fuming. Then, one boss had had enough.

"Pick 'em up and shoot 'em!" he roared, showing total disdain for the young shooter. But the shooter, with the whole table behind him, showed even more disdain for the boss: He completely ignored him. On and on he went, number after number, even getting some pointers from the high roller on exactly how to set those dice.

The shooter was after a hard 8. Everyone knew how the shooter was superstitiously prepping them bones, setting them up for a forty-four. "Fours on top," the table clamored, and fours on top they flew.

The high roller by now had gotten on the bandwagon and filled the hard-8 box with lots of black chips. He had all the other hardways covered, too, with several thousand dollars scattered around the table. It was bedlam; it was pandemonium. It was fun. Except for the bosses. "I'm going to tell you one more time. Shoot 'em; don't play with 'em!"

The shooter responded by adding a new twist to the routine. He'd kiss the dice just before they flew. Hey, this wasn't dice. This was in-your-face football. The shooter was on one side of the line, and the boss was on the other. And everyone knew the kid was like a young Montana, and the boss was "Mean Joe Greene."

"Six, 6 hard," calls the stickman. And a ton of money goes to the players.

"Close, very close," said the high roller.

"Nine, 9 in the field, 9." And the crowd lets out a sigh. After all, they're expecting hardways. Nothing but hard numbers.

The boss changes the stick, and the new stickman is quickly initiated: "Ten, 10 hard," he cries. And more chips go from dealers to players. Many more.

The shooter fumbles with the dice, looking for that forty-four, and the nervousness shows in his fingers, but not on his face. His look is of confidence. And everyone at the table knew the next number would be forty-four. If you don't understand that, then you're not a real dice player. There was no question in anyone's mind. The next roll would set the place on fire.

While the shooter was tapping the dice again, and starting his circular motion, the pit boss quietly motioned to the stickman to retrieve the dice. And with a scream that woke up all the bosses in the blackjack pit, the dice table's commander-in-chief said, "Pass 'em!"

"What? What does he mean? What the hell's going on here?" cried everyone at the table.

"New shooter," said the stickman in a calming but futile voice. "We have a new shooter going for the point of 8."

Need I tell you that the table turned hostile? But the big surprise was yet to come.

The high roller, who was standing beside the young man who had just lost the dice, launched a mortar attack on the boss: "How dare you treat my son like this? You'll be lucky to get a job on a riverboat when I get done with you."

"That's his son?" the boss mumbled to himself.

Well, the new shooter just stood there. He didn't know what to do. "Shoot the dice, sir," said the boss, nodding his head in an up-and-down "yes" motion. "Yeah, go ahead, shoot the damn things."

But before the new shooter could even reach for the dice, the high roller told him, "Don't pick 'em up. Don't even touch 'em."

The boss told the stickman to pass the dice again.

"Don't anyone shoot 'em," said the high roller. "My kid's gonna make that hard 8 or nobody is! Just let 'em pass around the table."

And pass they did. All the way back to the kid who had them taken away in the first place. Then past him again. The stickman just stood there staring at the boss. The dice were in the center of the table, a table that was in limbo. No one moved. No one even talked. It was a scene that reminded me of the old '50s movie, *The Day the Earth Stood Still.*

And then, as loud as he could proclaim, the high roller said, "WE WANT THE MANAGER!" And he said it again, and again. And the chant started, everyone joined in: "We want the manager, we want the manager!"

It didn't take long for the casino manager to come over.

"Who are you?" said the high roller.

"I'm the casino manager, and what the hell's going on here?"

"My son had the dice taken away from him."

The manager turned to the boss, and in a cracking voice I could hear the boss tell his boss, "Shit, Tony, I didn't know the kid was his son."

"Well," said Tony, whispering so no one could hear him, "Let's close the game and give the bets back. This could be ugly."

"What?" said the boss, "You can't do that! Every hand has to be played out. You know the rules…"

"Damn it, Sandy. Why do you get into these messes? Go to table 4 and watch that game."

"But there isn't a game on table 4. Table 4's closed."

"I know."

And off went the perpetrator, the pit boss, the pit viper—the jerk.

The manager looked around and saw too many people gawking at him, not only from the table, but now people were in the aisles. The confrontation had become a sideshow. So he did what any intelligent—strike that—what any moron would do. He ordered the stickman to give the dice back to the kid, and then he told the boxman (the next level of authority at the table) to leave the kid alone. As the manager left the pit, the boxman jumped up from his chair and grabbed him. "Leave him alone? What do you mean? What if he doesn't hit the wall?"

"Wall? Shmall? I don't give a damn if he shoots 'em out of his nose. Just get the decision." (What he really meant, of course, was "just get me the 7.")

So the dice, sitting forlornly in the center of the table, got pushed back into action. And the kid shooter was ready to roll.

"Eight, son," reminded the high roller, "any old 8 will do."

The kid didn't fiddle with them as much as before, but he did throw them harder—a lot harder. One die hit a stack of chips, and the other went off spinning like a top, hiding behind the dealer's stacks of chips.

"I've got a 4 here," said the stickman, pointing to the die that everyone could see. But all eyes were trying to find the hidden die, the one that was still spinning. Everyone was sharing each other's thoughts: No, it couldn't be a 3. No way. 4. Yeah, 4. It's gotta be. It's justice.

Five. 5?

"Nine, 9 in the field, 9," bellows the stickman.

Everyone was so shocked, they thought they had just lost. But it was a number, and a very good number.

The kid continued to shoot for another ten minutes or so.

But he never made his 8.

Applause. Applause.

8 MORE INFORMATION

SIZING UP THE SHOOTER

Dice players have a dubious habit of trying to get a fix on a particular shooter, thinking to themselves, Is this guy gonna be okay, or is he a loser? And what about that woman beside him, what's she gonna do? Chronic dice players even keep mental notes on how well a particular shooter did the last time out. If a shooter made a lot of money for the players, and the dice are back in front of him, you'll hear comments buzzing around the table like, "Hey, this guy's good!" "Yeah, he had one helluva hot hand this morning!"

There was a story in the paper the other day about a chimpanzee who liked to shoot craps. So, one day, the zoo keepers decided to see just exactly how good this chimp really was! They gave him a new pair of casino-issue dice and set up a wall for the monkey to shoot against. Guess what? The chimp made eight straight passes! And you thought you were good!

What you just read is a good answer to a question I get all the time: How do I size up a shooter? The answer is: I don't. In fact, I make a special effort not to look at the shooter. It makes no difference to me who's shooting—except a mechanic, of course—because it makes no difference to the dice.

I just gave you the best case in point, but I have another one if you're still not convinced.

THIS BUD'S FOR YOU!

At the Las Vegas Hilton recently, I was stuck in a slow game with not much success, but I decided I would go one more shooter.

The dice dribble halfway down the table and make 6 the point. I load up the odds and toss three reds in the come. Slowly down the table come the dice again, barely making it to the wall, and my bet goes to the 8. Another come, another wimpy roll, and now I've got 9 working.

The stickman tells the shooter, "All the way to the end, sir," and here they come with force, crashing into the dealer's stacks of chips. "Ten, 10 easy," mumbles the stickman, while the dealer rolls his eyes and cleans up his chips.

Great. Now I've got more bets out there than I wanted, and I've got some idiot shooting who can't even hit the wall, much less roll them down the middle. I decide to glance down the table to see what this guy looks like, and it's all I can do to draw a bead on him—he's weaving all over the place while firmly holding onto the table as if he's hanging from the balcony on the 30th floor. This guy is so many sheets to the wind that I'm beginning to feel a little woozy myself. Here I am with a hundred and eighty bucks invested on this table and my money's in the hands of a drunk who can't even stand up.

The stickman calls "Dice are out," and out they go, over the table and through the woods, and clear over to grandma's house. I think he missed the entire table by thirty feet!

So, do I pull my odds, give the dealers the flats for a tip, and bail out? I look at the other players at my end of the table and we're all thinking the same thing: Here comes the 7!

No, actually, here comes one die; the other one remained in his hand. "It got stuck," he laughs, like a Foster Brooks routine. Now the bosses are getting a little edgy with this guy. "Look buddy, both dice, Okay? Both dice, nice and easy, down the center of the table. Can you do that for us?"

CRASH! Yes, another shot at the dealer's chip stacks. Only this time the impact is so severe that chips have rolled into the point boxes. And, not surprisingly, there's only one die to be seen, 6 it is. But where's the other cube? It's not in the shooter's hand because the drunk has both hands firmly on the table. Hmm. The other die is quickly found under a mess of chips. I'll save you the suspense. We all knew there would only be a one-spot on that die. I mean, there was no need to ponder. It was a given. This drunk would seven-out on us in the most pathetic exhibition I've ever witnessed.

Clearing away the mess of chips reveals the 4—what? A 4? Hell! That's my 10 he just made. That idiot just made my 10!

Then he made my 9!

Then he made my 8!

Then the point of 6!

Don't ask me how many more numbers he rolled, but I can tell you there were at least two more Budweisers in the equation.

Not a bad shoot for someone who won't remember a damn thing about it the next morning.

So, the next time you size up a shooter, remember the monkey and remember the drunk. And remember this: The dice are no respecters of the shooter. The dice have more important things to worry about.

GENTLEMEN, START YOUR ENGINES!

The Desert Inn in Las Vegas has been the scene of many of my most memorable dice-table stories. This particular story is a good lesson in jumping in. Or should I say, not jumping in. Dice tables are not pools. But some dice tables—to accommodate gutsy players we've all witnessed—should come equipped with diving boards.

All of us at the table that evening were certainly not high rollers, not by any stretch of the imagination. There were a few of us making green-chip bets, most though were red-chip bettors. The table was decent, and I had worked my pass line bets up to $75 or so. Nothing that was going to shake the foundations of this glorious hotel.

But this one notable gentleman had stood watch over the table for quite a while. We all saw him. Distinguished looking. A nice suit, silver hair, a perfectly folded handkerchief in his coat pocket. I'm sure you can picture him as well as I remember him. Thinking the table was warming up, which it kind of was, he took a spot at the table that seemed reserved for him. We all knew the next thing to happen. The stickman held back the dice as a courtesy to the new player, awaiting his command—a dice game's equivalent of "Gentlemen, start your engines."

"Give me five thousand," says the high roller, in his most serious of expressions, followed quickly by his acknowledging smile to each of us at the table. Now his table.

Five hundred on the pass line and off go the dice to begin mounting a pile of money for this roller of all rollers who did exactly what he is supposed to do. He watched. He waited. He found what he liked. He played.

And we played. Building up a nice pile of money, too, but in a drastically different color.

All of a sudden the game stops again. Mr. High Roller has just plunked down five-thousand dollars on the pass line. His own specially approved limit, no doubt, because the posted limit is two thousand.

Off go the dice again to the point of 4.

"You can take ten thousand in odds, Mr. B," says the dealer, noting that "Mr. B" had paused for a moment, somewhat bewildered, because he didn't have it, at least not all of it, to put down. He could muster only five thousand in his chip tray. But a quick scan of the table showed that he did have it, but it was all in play—at least another five thousand was sitting on the table in come bets. We could all figure it out in our heads. He started with five grand, he had five grand in profit to put down in odds, and at least another five grand spread on the table. Wow! This guy is up ten grand!

"Well," Mr. B confesses, "I guess I'll need another five thousand so I can take full odds."

"Give it to him," says the floorman, making a mental note that he's now got two markers that will need to be signed.

The chips, five pretty pink ones, join the other five pretty pink ones behind the line in what would be one heck of a nice payoff on a 4. Any 4. Because Mr. B doesn't care if it comes easy or comes hard. It just has to come. That's all. And if anything can bring it out, ten pretty pink ones ought to do it.

Down the table they go. Two red cubes in a blur of motion that cannot, will not, spit in the gentleman's face.

"Seven out," cries the stickman. "Line away," as his voice fades.

We're stunned.

A couple of players begin to applaud the shooter. After all, it was a good shoot. And then we all applaud as we get back to reality. All of us, that is, except Mr. B.

Through a smile as sincere as the one he brought to the table, Mr. B wants to know:

"What are you all applauding for? I just lost ten-thousand dollars!"

THE QUARTER TABLE

Who says you can't have fun playing craps? Who says you have to risk a lot of money to have fun? Who says you have to win to have fun? Pretend you're at this table: It's 7:15 a.m. and I'm early for a breakfast meeting at a local's joint just off the Strip in Vegas. No one who lives in Vegas wants to meet anywhere on the Strip for anything! You wanna meet, you meet somewhere out there where the real city is. And that's not Las Vegas Boulevard!

So here I am, and the place is pretty much dead except for a few slot machines cranking, and one lonesome dice table that seems to be making most of the noise in this place.

As I walked up, I hear some pretty heavy action going on:

"Quarter yo, Jerry."

"Yeah, give me a quarter yo, too, and a quarter any," says his buddy.

"Quarter each, all the hardways," says another, with chips aplenty in his hoard.

Yes sir! This was one Hilton-quality dice game going on where I would have least expected it.

As I walked up a little closer, I noticed the pit boss was a friend of mine from a big Strip casino.

"My God, Mike, why are you hangin' in a place like this? You belong back at the Dunes. Oh, yeah, I forgot, no more Dunes."

"Best thing that could have happened to me. Good, decent customers over here, John. No big stuff. No big-money games that used to drive me crazy. I like the pace here. I like the people."

"No big-money games?"

"Right."

"Hell, I'm seeing quarter chips all over the place and on prop bets yet. I'd call that big money. You've got some green-chip action like I've never seem before."

"They're just quarters."

"Yeah, I know, what is this, a quarter table? I don't even play that heavy anymore."

"Don't get cute, John. You can't get much smaller than these bets over here. We've got quarter action."

"Quarters?"

"Yeah. Quarter quarters."

"It's too early for me, Michael. I'm gonna go eat."

"Come on back when you're done, John. Ever played at a twenty-five cent game?"

"Twenty-five cents? I thought…"

"Oh, by the way, John, no markers, you know."

"No markers? You mean I can't write a marker for a couple bucks? That would probably last me the morning. Hey, Mike, I'm confused, if a quarter chip's a quarter, what's a nickel chip?"

"We don't have nickel chips, John. Couldn't make any money with nickel chips."

"Right."

"Come on back, John."

After breakfast, I did go back.

And I had fun.

I lost five dollars, and it seemed like five hundred!

That was fun!

THE WRONG TABLE

Casino gambling seems to attract a particular element that I've always been just a little uncomfortable with. Dice tables, for some reason, are the crowning example. Too often, when I tell a dice story, it always involves some jerk who either screws

up the game, or makes it unbearable for his neighbors. Case in point:

At the Dunes Hotel, years ago, I'm standing at the left corner of a fast-paced table enjoying a nice hand and helping a petite Asian woman standing beside me to my right. She didn't understand the game very well and wanted help. The dealers were too busy to assist her, the guy to her right was too busy loading up the table, so it was up to me to explain the game. Out of nowhere comes this idiot who barges right in between us, literally pushing the young lady away from the table.

"She's playing here. There's no room for you. Now back out," I told him.

His response was to basically tell me to mind my own business. He did open up a little space for the woman to reach in and at least put her hand around her chips in the tray, doing her best to hold on to her spot, but she had no way to see what's going on.

Now comes the fun.

The guy who had been standing to her right was fuming. He stepped back so that everyone could see him. And he was huge. I mean HUGE! He looks at the jerk who barged his way in and says, "You know what you are? You are an asshole! And you know what I'm going to do with you? I'm going to pull you apart, and one piece is going that way, and the other piece is going this way!"

Well, by now the pit had alerted security to a possible player confrontation, and they arrived in the nick of time. To watch, that is. They only stood there in awe and watched as this pushy, puny, punk of a man goes flying over the table. Literally. He had to be in the air for at least five seconds.

What was neat about this incident is that everyone cheered for the big guy. And the table never stopped, even while the jerk was being launched. The dice were in the air the same time he was!

Hey, this was more fun than a ringside seat for Tyson/ Holyfield. I've only seen a few real fights at a dice table, in spite of some of the sawdust joints I've played in. This was a classy fight, in a classy hotel, and to top it off, the table was hot! Who could ask for more ACTION?

After things simmered down, the pit boss came over to the table and said that the big guy was actually the Asian lady's boyfriend. And they had just returned from Maui, where he had won the All-Hawaiian Sumo Wrestling Championship.

Pity the poor jerk who picked the wrong table to crash. But, if the wrestler did to him what he said he was going to do, the next time he'll be able to barge into two tables at the same time!

I wonder if he can still take double odds.

OFF THE STRIP

My only other experience like that, actually a near miss, happened in Vegas at a small, off-the-Strip casino. I would never go to a place like that, but this friend who was with me knew a dealer there. We found an empty dice table (they were all empty) and started playing. Within minutes, every drunk in the entire city of Las Vegas was at that same table. I swear, they came out of the woodwork. And my friend, Jeff, decided he wanted to play as aggressively as he had been playing at the Mirage, with black chips.

The table was passing, so at least he had the right idea, just the wrong casino. You see, the problem was that the casino didn't have any black chips, at least not at that table. So, all of his payoffs were in green. It made it look like Jeff was breaking the casino. We assumed the dusty green chips were there just to look at, reserved for the casino's, uh, "high rollers." The other players who had joined us paid more attention to Jeff's bets

than to their own dollar-this, dollar-that. Jeff, unknowingly, or uncaringly, was making a spectacle of himself.

It was an hour later when we decided to blow this dump, and the trip to the casino cage was rather eventful. I helped him carry his stacks and stacks of greenies but my hands were full, too, so we put them in our pockets, under our hats, in our shorts—well, you get the picture. Standing around us was every single one of those drunks. We figured they just wanted to see how much Jeff had won.

The nice lady at the cage was totally confused when she saw all of the chips. Her first response was, "What are these?" She gave us one of those pop-eyed expressions as if Jeff had dropped his pants. If he would have, we would have found more chips! Anyway, it took the better part of a half hour to count those suckers. She was all butterfingers with at least three other butterfingers standing behind her recounting what she had just counted. The whole scene played like a Three Stooges movie.

And you guessed it. As we walked out of the place, all the drunks followed us. Jeff looked back as we reached the front door and commented that not all of those jokers were the drunks; there were at least half-a-dozen casino bosses right behind us.

What to do. What to do.

I noticed a cab stuck in traffic right in front of the casino. I think we both noticed it at the same time, and made a beeline for it. The cabbie had a fare in the backseat and wouldn't take us, so we gave him a C-note and he got out and opened the door for us. Now that's the kind of treatment we should expect in Vegas. First class! Jeff gave him another hundred and said, "Get us out of here!" The cabbie, looking around, with no place to go (there was stalled traffic in every lane) made like a New York City cab driver—no, make that Mario Andretti, the racecar driver—and got us out of there like a rocket. The cabbie's customer, an older gentleman, looked at us as if we had just robbed the casino.

"You didn't, uh, you didn't, uh..."

"Yeah, we did."

BIG FISH, LITTLE FISH

The larger casinos employ hosts to take care of their premium players. Hosts are like valets; they cater to every whim of the high roller. And if the high roller just happens to be the highest of the high rollers (casinos call them **whales**), the situation can be a totally subservient role for the poor host, running the gamut from slave to pimp. To make matters worse, many examples of this rather large species have been known to make life miserable for the host. Here's one side of an exchange between a Vegas host and a Dallas bigwig:

"Good morning, sir. Is everything to your liking? Is there anything I can do for you? Palm Springs? Your wife wants to go shopping in Palm Springs? Yes, absolutely, I'll have a limo ready immediately, sir. You know, that's a five-hour drive. Your wife won't be back until this evening. Oh, I get it! Very good, sir. Yes, the girls will be at your door at noon.

"Mushrooms? I heard about that, sir. I've instructed room service not to put mushrooms on your salad.

"The fruit basket? Not enough pears? Our computer file indicated you don't like pears. More pears. Absolutely, sir.

"Door slamming? Yes, I heard about that, too, sir. I've asked our hotel manager to move out all the other guests around your suite.

"Towels? Let's see, yes, I have that here, sir. The pool attendant has already been dismissed. I'm sorry about the way he treated you, sir."

For the record, this guy's name is on the wait staff's list of the most hated guests of the hotel. Everyone can't wait till the day he leaves. And they dread the day he returns. But the comptroller likes him. The casino cleans up on this guy. For a little ass-kissing, they rake in a cool hundred grand at the tables.

In the casino, your mega-money can buy instant respect. But it's as empty as that fake smile that greets you at the door.

"Nice to see you again, sir."

Nice to see you again, my ass.

At the other end of the spectrum are the guy and his wife who are a joy to the casino employees. They're friendly to everyone and always smiling. But their action at the tables produces only a modest win for the casino. Here's both sides of the conversation between player and host when he called to make reservations:

"You want what? You were overcomped on your last stay by $147. The trip before that by $250. And the trip before that we gave you $180 in comps that you didn't earn. What do you take us for, a bunch of morons? You've conned us three times in a row."

"Oh, no! I'm not trying to con anyone. My wife and I play a lot, and you've always provided a nice room for us before."

"Well, we've got new management now, and this ain't no soup line."

"Okay, then just give us a casino rate on the room."

"No can do."

"Okay, just take our reservations, then. We like your hotel and…"

"Can't do that."

"What? I can't even get a reservation?"

"No. We've got a blackjack tournament going on over that weekend, and besides, we have to keep a number of rooms available for our premium players. You'll have to stay someplace else."

"We will!"

So what's behind this strangely discriminatory way of treating casino guests? Is there some kind of code that pops up on the computer screen when the host punches in the player's name? Perhaps it's a fish code: High rollers might be coded as a shark, or a whale, or—in the case of our first example—a barracuda. Low rollers could be anything from a sunfish to a minnow. I wouldn't be surprised if some casinos have programmed their computers so that little fish icons are displayed beside the name. Those icons will tell the host whether to talk nasty or nice, or something in between. Maybe starting out nice, and finishing up nasty.

What's really behind it? Seriously? Well, for one thing— and I know this won't come as any great shock to you—but the world of casino gambling is full of Great Pretenders. It's up to the hosts of the world to separate the play money from the real money.

And there really is an issue of just exactly how big a fish you are. If you live in a little pond back home, don't expect comped gourmet meals. You may be the gourmet meal.

Another reason is a bit philosophical, I suppose, but I've always believed that gambling tends to bring out the worst in people. Particularly those who work in it. Just being around it seems to have a hardening effect on one's basic civility. Probably because of money. Money everywhere. Easy money. Having it, or not having it, tops the casino's distorted list of values.

Whatever the reason, casinos have a new corporate creation, Player Development, responsible for stocking the pond. Indeed, the real aim of this department is to separate players into two distinct groups: big fish and little fish. But, to me, it seems like a waste of time devising this sinister food chain. Because it really doesn't matter, in the long run, which you are. Whether

you're treated nicely or rudely. Whether you dine on steak or hamburgers. Whether you bet big or bet little.

Why doesn't it matter? Because the casino is just nibbling on you.

Just before they eat you.

FOUR-LETTER WORDS

A tableful of colorful players, and me, colorful to the extent I had a blue shirt on, and we're all taking it on the chin from a very strong blackjack dealer. I've never heard such colorful language in my life. In fact, it got so bad that a lady pit boss came over to our table and really bawled us out for using those choice 4-letter words reserved for sailors. She looked at me, too, as she pointed that school teacher finger. Guilty by association, I guess.

These other players were betting big, and losing in ways that would make the Pope cuss. I'm talking nice pat 20s losing to a dealer's 5-card draw to 21! I'm talking dealer stiffs, one after another, turning into 19s and 20s. Why didn't everyone move? Because everyone, it seemed, was dealt winning hands. Or should I say, hands that should have won?

Cussing at this table was perfectly acceptable under the circumstances—I mean, what did the lady boss expect?

"Gosh, Mr. Blackjack Dealer. That was a fine five-card 21 you just made to beat my 20. Never mind the fact I doubled down on a hundred bucks. Well, shoot, I guess that stuff just happens. Well, sir, I think I'll try my luck at another table. Good day, sir. It was nice meeting you."

I don't think so. There were no Eddie Haskells at this table. No smiles, either, but a lot of threatening looks.

So off to the dice tables I go, mumbling a few choice words that I picked up from a golfing buddy of mine who just yesterday was taking wicked swipes at his hacked-up golf ball, as if to punish it for finding every sand trap on the course. If there was a trap on the hole, my buddy would find it. I told him the next time he wants to practice, all he has to do is go down to the beach. It was a round of golf that could only be described with the most vulgar, most offensive 4-letter words that would embarrass an Atlantic City cab driver. Yes indeed, I learned some choice words from that experience and today I had found the perfect opportunity to use them.

By the middle of the day, I was playing my 9th hour at the dice tables for this trip, without even a hint of a hot shoot. It was three o'clock. My last day. My last chance. My limo was to pick me up at five.

The dice passed quickly by my end of the table and on down to an old geezer in a red baseball cap. I told the player to my right that this guy was going to have a hell of a hand. Then I told the guy to my left. We had a few words earlier and I didn't want to talk to him because he tried to claim a come bet of mine. It was my come, not his, but the stupid dealer just stood there, shrugging his shoulders, while this guy is trying to lay claim to my quarter 10 with $50 odds that just hit! Here's the gist of that conversation:

"Hey, wait a minute," I told him. "You can't use swear words like that at a dice table. I have it on good authority that people are not allowed to swear in this casino."

"Oh yeah?"

"Yeah!"

I don't know where it would have ended had it not been for the boxman who said, "No sir, it's the gentleman in the blue shirt (me) who made that bet. You, sir, had a come bet that went to the 4."

How polite.

Of course that didn't satisfy him. He still thought I collected on his bet. So why would I even look at him, let alone

strike up a conversation with him? Why would I put myself in such an awkward position as to predict the hot shoot that was about to come?

Because I knew.

"Yeah, right." That's all he said.

The shooter proceeded to make a hero out of me. The longer he threw, the louder the accolades. "This guy predicted it," said the player to my right. The dealer even got involved. "Yeah, how did you know that? Especially the way the table's going. You really put yourself on the spot. But you were right."

The consummate swearer next to me was all smiles. But he was still swearing. We'll call it "happy swearing."

So how did I do? From upside down a thousand in markers to cashing in five thousand in chips, all in about 30 minutes. And that's the way the game is played.

While standing at the cashier's cage, I remembered I had a pocketful of reds and greens. I had planned to give them to the dealers as a tip, but I forgot. So, I figured, on the way to the front door, I'll run by and toss the reds on the table for the dealers. But I remembered how unimpressed I was with this particular crew. And, as the cashier counted out over a hundred in "tip" chips, I decided to head straight for the door.

And there was my limo. On time.

So the driver got a nice tip.

I swear.

JUST HANGIN'

I like to mix my gambling when I'm in Vegas, because there I have many more opportunities than in any other gaming market. Here are the areas of a casino where I like to hang around when I'm in Vegas, besides the dice tables. They represent what I believe are the best opportunities for long-term potential.

I only stay at a casino with an outstanding race and sports book. I believe that a good sports bettor can easily overcome the juice and show some consistency in win revenue. In that same comfy edifice, one can play the ponies. Although horse racing is largely a dying institution, the potential for a good handicapper is still there. I only recommend the major tracks, however, and that's what's nice about the race books in Nevada: For the most part, only the major tracks are carried. Indeed, horse racing is the other form of wagering that I think lends itself to a long-term potential.

There's another spot in the casino worth mentioning. It's where a good player isn't good enough, but a damn good one is. It's the poker parlor. If you think you're good, you're not; if Doyle Brunson thinks you're good, you're damn good. And if that's the case, you can sit back, relax, and wait for the next busload, or planeload, of suckers to come in.

Believe it. There are some poker players, there are some sports bettors, and there are some horse players who can put food on the table.

Experts? Yeah. They're experts.

THE GOLDEN GOOSE

As far as the skill elements of gambling are concerned, especially as they apply to blackjack, I've found that players in the great majority are not interested in developing any measurable skill. Either they don't want to take the time and effort, or they simply pretend they have a skill. So who's kidding whom?

Blackjack is one of five games in a Nevada casino where skill is an absolute must. The same can be said for video poker (the

machine), but skill at this game is not enough to consistently overcome the percentages in most of the games offered. The others we just talked about are poker (the live game), horse racing in the casino's race book, and sports betting in the casino's sports book.

We now know that the skill element at the dice tables can produce significant results, but with a nasty downside. Indeed, dice mechanics are not playing by the rules. But there's an interesting aside to that. Craps has seen some modest revitalization over the years. But overall, the game needs a shot in the arm. When I did an interview just before this book was released, I talked about the possibility that some "skill" shots might be worth legalizing in order to pump up the game. There's no question that dice, like roulette, needs something to perk up interest.

What perked up the interest in blackjack decades ago was all the talk—not to mention all the books that came out—about basic strategy and card counting. The fervor set off tidal waves of interest. Finally, there was a casino game that could be beaten with a skill.

The discovery of a basic strategy for blackjack—and later, a powerful card-counting strategy—accomplished something that casino bosses, even today, won't acknowledge: It gave blackjack great popularity. Players from everywhere zeroed in on their favorite casino to test their skill. New players were cultivated in ranks never seen before.

The casino bosses, instead of being happy with all the new action they were getting, took their own defensive action and nearly killed the Golden Goose. Casino executives, paranoid people that they are, feared that every single player would knock 'em out. How stupid. Any moron should have been able to figure out that only a minuscule percentage of these new-wave players would actually have the skill necessary to beat them. All the other players would easily make up for the less than one-tenth of one percent who could actually beat the game.

Rule changes and countermeasures were all that had to be done to soften the blow. If it had been marketed right, these changes would not have had the negative impact that caused many players to quit the game. Plainly, the casino hierarchy overreacted. Player intimidation, bullying, and threats of arrest were enough to chase off the great majority of new players, most of whom posed no threat to the casino in the first place. I've always believed that if the casino owners had their marketing people call the shots at this critical stage, instead of the old-line casino managers, the game would have maintained most of its heyday levels.

Today, there's a growing disinterest in blackjack. The game is very difficult to beat. And, not surprisingly, many disenchanted blackjack players are hearing the noise from the dice tables and venturing over. You might be surprised at how many new dice players are former blackjack players who no longer feel they can break even, let alone win. Like I said, the game has been overtoughened.

Which brings us back to dice and the issue of dice mechanics: If the industry regulators were to consider legalizing certain skill tosses, just think of the interest it would create. There would be an even greater fervor than what happened decades ago, because the pool of players has grown tenfold since that time. Of course, the blatant slide-shot and scoot-shot could not be legalized. That's cheating, plain and simple. But what about the spin-shots, where a true skill is required and, like card counting, is not a skill of absolute certainty? It's a skill that has to be mastered. Few people, probably that same less than one-tenth of one percent, would be able to do it.

Unfortunately, there's one big problem with this argument: Card counting benefits the individual player whereas a dice spinner would benefit the entire table, assuming that everyone's

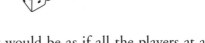

betting with the shooter. It would be as if all the players at a blackjack table put all their bets in the card counter's circle.

I can see it happening. "Hey, Phil, what's with all these players spinning the dice?"

"Yeah, I know. Some jerk wrote a book about dice mechanics, and now everyone is trying it."

So, up goes the sign over every dice table, "NO SPIN-SHOTS." And history will again repeat itself. The casino bosses will have overreacted.

9 CONCLUSION

Winning at craps demands that you have confidence in your strategy. I hope that this book has helped you do exactly that, play with ease and confidence, knowing that you are using the best strategies to win every time you put your money on the table.

Craps is a game that can empty the pockets of players who do not have the knowledge that you have learned in this book. The temptation to bet all of the exotic yet terrible bets overwhelms them in the heat of the action. Such a player is a pure gambler, not the level-headed, informed player this book has helped you become.

The real thrill of the game is winning, and the greatest thrill of all is winning big! With the powerful strategies I've armed you with in this book, you are now able to protect your bankroll if you face a bad streak—and crush the house when the dice go your way.

Bet sensibly and manage your money wisely. Have fun. Combine all this with smart play and you'll be a winner!

Win at Blackjack Without Counting Cards!!!
Multiple Deck 1, 2, 3 Non-Counter - Breakthrough in Blackjack!!!

BEAT MULTIPLE DECK BLACKJACK WITHOUT COUNTING CARDS!

You heard right! Now, for the **first time ever**, **win** at multiple deck blackjack **without counting cards**! Until I developed the Cardoza Multiple Deck Non-Counter (the 1,2,3 Strategy), I thought it was impossible. Don't be intimidated anymore by four, six or eight deck games—for **you have the advantage**. It doesn't matter how many decks they use, for this easy-to-use and proven strategy keeps you **winning—with the odds**!

EXCITING STRATEGY—ANYONE CAN WIN! -

We're **excited** about this strategy for it allows anyone at all, against any number of decks, to have the **advantage** over any casino in the world in a multiple deck game. You don't count cards, you don't need a great memory, you don't need to be good at math - you just need to know the **winning secrets** of the 1,2,3 Multiple Deck Non-Counter and use but a **little effort** to win $$$.

SIMPLE BUT EFFECTIVE! -

Now the answer is here. This strategy is so **simple**, yet so **effective**, you will be amazed. With a **minimum of effort**, this remarkable strategy, which we also call the 1,2,3 (as easy as 1,2,3), allows you to win without studiously following cards. Drink, converse with your fellow players or dealer - they'll never suspect that you can **beat the casino**!

PERSONAL GUARANTEE -

And you have my personal **guarantee of satisfaction**, 100% money back! This breakthrough strategy is my personal research and is guaranteed to give you the edge! If for any reason you're not satisfied, send back the materials unused within 30 days for a full refund.

BE A LEISURELY WINNER! -

If you just want to play a **leisurely game** yet have the expectation of winning, the answer is here. Not as powerful as a card counting strategy, but **powerful enough to make you a winner** - with the odds!!!

EXTRA BONUS! -

Complete listing of all options and variations at blackjack and how they affect the player. ($5.00 Value!)

EXTRA, EXTRA BONUS!! -

Not really a bonus since we can't sell you the strategy without protecting you against getting barred. The 1,000 word essay, "How to Disguise the Fact That You're an Expert," and the 1,500 word "How Not To Get Barred," are also included free. ($15.00 Value)

To order, send ~~$75~~ $50 (plus postage and handling) by check or money order to:
Cardoza Publishing, P.O. Box 98115, Las Vegas, NV 89193

WIN MONEY AT BLACKJACK! SPECIAL OFFER!
THE CARDOZA BASE COUNT STRATEGY

Finally, a count strategy has been developed which allows the average player to play blackjack like a **pro**! Actually, this strategy isn't new. The Cardoza Base Count Strategy has been used successfully by graduates of the Cardoza School of Blackjack for years. But **now**, for the **first time**, this "million dollar" strategy, which was only available previously to those students attending the school, is available to **you**!

FREE VACATIONS! A SECOND INCOME? - You bet! Once you learn this strategy, you will have the skills to **consistently win big money** at blackjack. The longer you play, the more you make. The casino's bankroll is yours for the taking.

BECOME AN EXPERT IN TWO DAYS - Why struggle over complicated strategies that aren't as powerful? In just **two days or less**, you can learn the Cardoza Base Count and be among the best blackjack players. Friends will look up to you in awe - for you will be a **big winner** at blackjack.

BEAT ANY SINGLE OR MULTIPLE DECK GAME - We show you how, with just a **little effort**, you can effectively beat any single or multiple deck game. You'll learn how to count cards, how to use advanced betting and playing strategies, how to make money on insurance bets, and much more in this 6,000 word, chart-filled strategy package.

SIMPLE TO USE, EASY TO MASTER - You too can win! The **power** of the Cardoza Base Count strategy is not only in its **computer-proven** winning results but also in its **simplicity**. Many beginners who thought card counting was too difficult have given the Cardoza Base Count the acid test - they have **won consistently** in casinos around the world. The Cardoza Base Count strategy is designed so that **any player** can win under practical casino conditions. **No need** for a mathematical mind or photographic memory. **No need** to be bogged down by calculations. Keep **only one number** in your head at any time. The casinos will never suspect that you're a counter.

DOUBLE BONUS!! - **Rush** your order in **now**, for we're also including, **absolutely free**, the 1,000 and 1,500 word essays, "How to Disguise the Fact that You're an Expert", and "How Not to Get Barred". Among other **inside information** contained here, you'll learn about the psychology of the pit bosses, how they spot counters, how to project a losing image, role playing, and other skills to maximize your profit potential.

As an **introductory offer to readers of this book**, the Cardoza Base Count Strategy, which has netted graduates of the Cardoza School of Blackjack **substantial sums** of **money**, is offered here for **only** $50!

To order, send $50 by check or money order to:
Cardoza Publishing, P.O. Box 98115, Las Vegas, NV 89193

THE CARDOZA CRAPS MASTER

Exclusive Offer! - Not Available Anywhere Else)

Three Big Strategies!

Here It is! **At last**, the **secrets** of the **Grande-Gold Power Sweep, Molliere's Monte Carlo Turnaround** and the **Montarde-D'Girard Double Reverse** - three big strategies - are made available and presented for the **first time anywhere!** These powerful strategies are designed for the serious craps player, one wishing to bring the best odds and strategies to hot tables, cold tables and choppy tables.

1. THE GRANDE-GOLD POWER SWEEP (HOT TABLE STRATEGY)

This **dynamic strategy** takes maximum advantage of hot tables and shows you how to amass small **fortunes quickly** when numbers are being thrown fast and furious. The Grande-Gold stresses aggressive betting on wagers the house has no edge on! This previously unreleased strategy will make you a powerhouse at a hot table.

2. MOLLIERE'S MONTE CARLO TURNAROUND (COLD TABLE STRATEGY)

For the player who likes betting against the dice, Molliere's Monte Carlo Turnaround shows how to turn a cold table into hot cash. Favored by an exclusive circle of professionals who will play nothing else, the uniqueness of this strongman strategy is that the vast majority of bets **give absolutely nothing away to the casino!**

3.MONTARDE-D'GIRARD DOUBLE REVERSE (CHOPPY TABLE STRATEGY)

This **new** strategy is the **latest development** and the **most exciting strategy** to be designed in recent years. **Learn how** to play the optimum strategies against the tables when the dice run hot and cold (a choppy table) with no apparent reason. **The Montarde-d'Girard Double Reverse** shows how you can **generate big profits** while less knowledgeable players are ground out by choppy dice. And, of course, the majority of our bets give nothing away to the casino!

BONUS!!!

Order now, and you'll receive **The Craps Master-Professional Money Management Formula** ($15 value) **absolutely free!** Necessary for serious players and **used by the pros**, the **Craps Master Formula** features the unique **stop-loss ladder.**

The Above Offer is Not Available Anywhere Else. You Must Order Here.

To order send $75 $50 (plus postage and handling) by check or money order to:
Cardoza Publishing, P.O. Box 98115, Las Vegas, NV 89193